Intervention

Intervention

Course Corrections for the Athlete and Trainer

Dan John

Foreword
Thomas Plummer

On Target Publications
Santa Cruz, California

Intervention
Course Corrections for the Athlete and Trainer

Dan John
Foreword: Thomas Plummer

Copyright © 2013, Daniel Arthur John
ISBN-13: 978-1-931046-17-6

On Target Publications
P. O. Box 1335
Aptos, CA 95001 USA
(888) 466-9185
info@otpbooks.com
www.otpbooks.com

Library of Congress Cataloging-in-Publication Data
      John, Dan.
        Intervention : course corrections for the athlete and trainer / Dan
      John ;
       foreword, Thomas Plummer
          p. cm.
       Includes index.
       ISBN 978-1-931046-17-6 (pbk.)
       1. Weight lifting. 2. Weight training. 3. Bodybuilding. 4. Physical
      education and training. I. Title.
       GV546.3.J64 2013
       613.7'1301--dc22
                                        2013012888

For
Heath Robinson
Father, Husband, Friend, SEAL
KIA 2011, Afghanistan

Acknowledgements

A FEW YEARS AGO, at Mike Boyle's Winter Seminar in Boston, a dark-haired man in glasses came up to me and said, "You live in San Francisco. I live in San Francisco." With that began my relationship with Steve Ledbetter, also known as Coach Stevo. Stevo's contributions to this work can't be ignored; he is a friend, confidant and companion on the journey.

Stevo went all in with the concept of Intervention in its earliest form. He continued to ask the questions and prod for more depth about all the points. His adoption of the protocols and principles expanded in this book gave feedback about the needs for more clarity and more focus.

Stevo is an early adopter of Intervention and has walked many clients through this process. His experiences—and frustrations—are found in the four sidebar stories spread throughout the book. He also took on the task of showing how our basic human movements expand far beyond the weightroom into the areas of throwing, which, in hindsight, should have been much more obvious to me. Stevo's contributions to the field of fitness continue to grow, and I hope I get partial credit for "discovering him."

In a way, I am honored to work with such fine young men like Coach Stevo and my other contributor, Tim Anderson. Tim's work on resetting the body is life-changing, and I am perhaps his best example of this approach. It makes me happy to think I continue the legacy of Coach Ralph Maughan and Dick Notmeyer in impacting the future of fitness by giving a hand up to such fine young men. The future of the fitness industry seems solid with this new generation of coaches.

As always, I thank Tiffini, Kelly, Lindsay and Andrew for their ongoing support and patience as I continue to funnel enormous houseguests, hungry dinner companions and smelly bodies through their amazing lives.

Finally, I would be remiss if I didn't highlight and underline the impact and influence of Laree Draper on this project. On Target Publications has changed my life for the better and I think the world is a better place because of OTP.

Contents

Part 2

Foreword

THE STACK OF BOOKS, DVDs and articles people send me to review has become a never-finished pile strategically placed in the corner of my office. Years ago I simply gave up any timely review of most of these often-random works that represent everything in fitness from the rare and truly genius to the much more common worthless material that should never see the light of day or find its way to any fitness professional's bookshelf.

I first met Dan John through this pile. I was leaving for a cross-country flight and picked up an unopened package from Laree Draper that contained Dan's latest book at the time, *Never Let Go*, threw it in my backpack and forgot about it. Finding myself wide awake on the plane and searching for something to read, I decided to give this new author a try.

Several hours later I finished the book, which was an apparent relief to those around me who found my endless laughter and obsessive note-taking somewhat of a nuisance during the five-hour flight. Dan had me at the cover, and I became so enthralled that I read the entire thing again on the return flight.

While Dan has always been sort of a rumpled rock star in the coaching world, only recently has he found his way into more mainstream fitness and is currently one of the most discussed and respected gurus in modern training. His following is ever-growing and he now enjoys a huge fan base amongst educated trainers and those working in the mainstream fitness world.

Much of this rising popularity is based upon Dan's perfect timing. The training world has grown weary over the years of quick-fix, one-trick masters who preach and scream the new gospel that ultimately fails, leaving a jaded and more cynical fitness professional. The era of "my way or the highway" leadership is tiring, yet there is still a need for leadership and clear thinking in the fast growing world of training.

Dan has provided that leadership through his previous writing and workshops and now with his newest book, *Intervention*. This book places him at the top echelon of teaching and thought in our field, along with other mind-changers such as Gray Cook, Alwyn Cosgrove, Mark Verstegen, Greg Rose, Rachel Cosgrove, Todd Durkin and Mike Boyle—all men and women who have helped us sort through the endless stream of nonsense to find what works, what is safe and what is necessary to train any athlete or regular client who simply wants to live a healthier and more fit life.

The current fitness world is in great turmoil. The mainstream box fitness players are failing and the next generation of training-centric businesses is rising. Much of this failing can be traced to one simple thought: Most of the accepted principles of modern fitness that were made popular by equipment companies and the false gurus selling their products and solutions just does not get sustainable results for our clients and athletes. This, coupled with a more educated consumer, has forced anyone working in fitness or coaching to reassess what works, what doesn't and where we should be going.

Dan's work helps us return to foundations of training by getting us to think about a return to the principles that have worked for literally hundreds of years, while introducing his current thought as to what he has learned through his decades of coaching, teaching and participating as a world-class athlete. His books forcefully get us to rethink everything we think we know about training and replace much of the "not needed" with plenty of the "can't live without."

As much as I like his work, his books are not what make Dan John important in our industry. Why I think he is a powerful role model for all trainers is not what he writes, which I find funny and often brilliant, but who he is and what he represents to all of us who work in this field.

The normal professional course for most trainers is to start out as a dangerous human with little practical knowledge, but with an enormous amount of theory and ideas as to how a person should be trained. Most new trainers agonize over the perfect workout, over-train virtually everyone and are the crazy purist idiots who embarrass themselves at restaurants trying to impress everyone with how clean they eat.

This is also why you should never eat dinner with trainers. It takes an hour to order the meal, as the trainer has to discuss types of oil, origin of meat, freshness of vegetables, and then humiliates the entire table as he whips out his own snack and organic mustard. We get it, you live pure; now order a big hunk of carcass, drink a good beer and just work out a little harder tomorrow. You will live and you will survive dinner out at 90% pure.

Luckily, the idiot stage only lasts a year or so and then the trainer moves into the hunger stage where he travels the world following the gurus, and spends hours with his other trainer friends discussing the latest Cosgrove post or Todd Durkin video. Every word is absorbed, every nuance copied, every book read, and he never misses a Perform Better Summit, or any other training agenda, where he can stalk his heroes and get the rare chance to ask questions and hang out with the Gods of fitness philosophy.

After that point, a few continue the quest for lifelong education, while most stagnate, trapped by their own successes. Develop a successful business, fill your life with clients and family and never again learn anything new. Over time, what you know is what you know and a new idea has as about as much of chance of getting through that dense head as a Twinkie getting eaten by the first-year purist.

Which brings us back to Dan.

Dan represents what we all should be, which is a seeker of what works, not only in training, but in life as well. His career and his life represent a never-ending search for how things work and how to not only be a good man in the classic sense, but also how to bring that trait out in others, which alone is something to make a life's work.

He also represents the best of what a man should be in that he is fair, humble, willing to help anyone who needs or wants his help, seeks a higher power through a lifelong career teaching students how to think about religion and higher power, and is not afraid to say he tried something, believed it for awhile, and then decided he was wrong and moves on.

Perhaps the trait he wears best, and this is probably the most important thing a young trainer should learn from him, is that over time we have to develop our own philosophies on training, and on life as well. Following gurus can help get us started on that trail, especially if we follow the honest men and women in the training world like those mentioned above. They're willing to do our thinking for us and they share the best and brightest information without arrogance and usually with patience and a drive to help others succeed.

I have watched Dan teach and am surprised at his patience to share without the need to always be right, another brutal trait of the young trainer who only knows his way or no way. Dan has spent a lifetime to finally get the recognition he deserves, yet he takes all the new attention and success as if he was on the side of the stage waiting for his turn to be called.

When I am asked about the future of the fitness business, I usually respond by stating that the big box membership era is on dangerous ground and that most of what we have presented to the public as fitness during the last several decades is failing. There is hope, however, and the future of our industry and the endurance of the common belief that what we do makes a difference in so many lives is safe, because change is coming from the trainer up. This change is being led by the best and brightest of this generation.

And of course, who is nurturing this new generation of leaders? It's the new hero, Dan John, and all the other gurus who are willing to share what they know and shape others' thoughts. Dan is, of course, a great read, but more importantly he would be what my father called a great man, defined by one who is willing to lead, to be wrong, and more importantly, to be right about the big things.

I hope you embrace this book and that you spend a lot of time getting to know Dan's work and getting to know him as a leader of this next generation.

Thomas Plummer
Author of *Making Money in the Fitness Business*
ThomasPlummer.com

PART

Chapter 1

Point A to Point B

IT TURNS OUT in the fitness world, I was the problem. Yes, this is true: I had great ideas, excellent programming and some nice technical tidbits that worked for everyone. For the squat, I had progressions I humbly think changed the world of lifting forever.

Well, at least I thought they were working. What I discovered was a disconnect: I was saying "this" and people were hearing "that." I thought I was making one point, but people were hearing another.

This reminds me of math class, by far my weakest subject.

"The shortest distance between two points is a straight line."

From Euclid…or, at least, what I can remember from geometry.

If you asked me to summarize all of this a few years ago, this entire system of what today I call *Intervention,* I would have been at a loss. Seriously, I had the whole thing locked down years and years ago, but there was disconnect, perhaps more of a gulf or an ocean, between what I thought I was saying and what people were hearing.

Honestly, the answer came to me just recently, a year after the *Intervention* DVD and the book *Mass Made Simple* came out, and after presenting this system to elite athletes, the top tier of coaches and amazing people who somehow "know" this is the future of the strength, conditioning and fitness world.

You see, this system is all about getting people to their goals. Now, as the cliché goes, "If you don't know where you're going, any road will get you there!"

This was the disconnect. I was expecting people to know where they were going because, for the most part, my career has been helping very serious people who knew exactly where they wanted to go: Olympics, Super Bowl, 10% body fat.

These people knew *exactly* where they wanted to go. And I got full of myself and became convinced this was the norm. But I had been working with 0.001% of the population. The other 99.999%, as I soon learned, had no concept of where they were heading, so my good advice was just another road for them to get lost on.

With the group who knew exactly where they were headed, I still think success is a straight line. I am sure you understand this: The fastest way from Point A, where you are, to Point B, where you want to go, is a straight line. My elite athletes always seem to know where they want to go—*Point B!!*

Here's the issue: They know about Point B. Point A, where they are right now, is a deep mystery.

Welcome to my approach to coaching those with clear goals. My simple vision is to identify where they are right now.

It's almost laughable to think about this, as most people would say, "Um, isn't that obvious? I'm right here!"

Then I laugh back. Really? And I add the old Irish joke, "I need to get to Dublin. Can you show me the way?"

"Well, I wouldn't start from here!"

After sitting with one of America's most elite service members and walking him through this system, he leaned back and smiled and asked, "What was I thinking? I am in a red light situation (he needed shrapnel pulled out of his back and leg, something I consider more important than competing in a fitness contest with no apparent rules), and I'm adding more crazy stress FOR NO REASON AT ALL!"

Yes, he shouted at me as if it were my fault! I have had people realize their short-term goals needed so many new skills, they just didn't have enough time in the day to learn all of the *stuff*.

The first problem is this: People were asking for my advice—my expensive advice—with no idea what they wanted to get from the conversation. So, and this is still true, I couldn't really help them.

I'm sorry, but if you're going to listen to every voice in the wind, I don't think I can be one of them. One can easily find a new diet and weight-loss idea every day of the week. As I often note, I didn't get enough food on that new diet, so now I am on two diets. If you don't know your goal, following two diets at once is probably just as good as anything I can encourage you to try.

This *Intervention* system is not for that person…yet. Oh, it will be, it will be (where is Yoda?). Once you know where you're going— your goal, your Point B—I can walk you through this system.

The approach, my friends, is all about discovering where you are. Now, since this is also the first question God asks Adam in *Genesis,* I have to be a little careful about treading on copyright violations. This, though, is the key to success.

Yes, it's important to have a goal so you can draw that straight line to it, but before we draw the line, we need to decide where to put the pencil in the first place.

With my elite athletes and trainees, we spend the bulk of our time discovering where they are—do they have the tools necessary for the goal? Do they have the skills, like a solid squat? Do they have the corrective movements mapped out, and know what needs to be corrected? Once we map out Point A, we discover a straight line. It might seem to be longer than the time allotted for the original goal, but now we can honestly begin walking down the path to success.

When I was in the ninth grade and first learning the discus, I read that an elite American thrower incline benchpressed 385 pounds. As I read it, I was doing the same move with 85 pounds. I knew A. I knew B. I knew exactly the road ahead of me and that was going to involve a lot of time in the weightroom.

And that's all fine. Elites aren't the problem; honestly, it's everyone else.

I have worked with some wonderful women who have the opposite issue, and the frankness brings them to tears.

"I am just so heavy…fat."

"I can't control this thing…and, (shaking an upper arm) what is this?"

"My husband won't touch me."

It is hard to hear, to be honest. But, this clarity about where they are, Point A, is stunning and just as real as the elite discus thrower who tells me she's going to the Olympics.

Welcome to the disconnect: Most people know Point A (I'm fat; I need to exercise and eat better), but Point B is the issue. These fine women see photoshopped images in fitness magazines and think that's Point B. You probably saw that recent set of before-and-after photos a young singer released—her legs got longer, her waist came in and her boobs got bigger...all in the artist's studio.

Folks, Point B is the issue for most of us. We're living in this odd time where fitness photos are dominated by hyperfit women with both genetic gifts and serious augmentation for the missing blanks and, frankly, this is not Point B for most people. It's Point Z!

Sadly, the fitness and fashion industries use Photoshop, vomiting and surgery to achieve the illusion of health and fitness. We need to slow down and show some reasonableness. We need to help people find their Point Bs.

So, here's our triple-edged sword that must be addressed.

- For whatever reason, some people, often athletes, see the goal clearly.
- Some people know exactly where they are physically, but need help seeing a realistic goal.
- There are others, of course, who are far from reality on either Point A or Point B, and we need to work both ends with them.

My whole career has been muddled by missing this point. This is why we need to do assessments early and often, like the Functional Movement Screen (FMS), "before" pictures (so you can "after"), basic strength tests and a few others. This is why we need to have food journals and some kind of proactive calendar efforts to let our clients know things are coming up that will impede progress or training, and some other things are easing up when we can accelerate to the goals.

We use these tools to answer the question, "Where are you?"

When Pavel Tsatsouline first introduced me to the concept of Easy Strength, the program freed up a lot of time, energy and intensity to allow me to work on the other qualities demanded of me as a thrower. I had the weightroom locked down, but needed more correctives (I'm Mr. Asymmetrical, Novice Class, Open Division) and to address some technical throwing issues.

When I work with almost everyone, fixing poor squat technique and the total lack of loaded carries makes a difference in their bodies and in their ability to train longer almost overnight. For some people like me, *Easy Strength*—or simple strength—answers the question of how to get to Point B more easily by just getting stronger.

But we need to assess to find Point A! Some will need focused time in the weightroom literally retooling and reschooling the issues so we can get back to the issues of technique, tactics and all the other tools.

With our friends who have no vision of where to go besides those celebrity diets that invade the grocery checkout line, we need to define a reasonable path to success. It might be food preparation, shopping skills, movement issues or whatever. It also includes realistic next steps and, even more importantly, realistic goals.

Get your people on the road to some Point B until they have the confidence to let Point Z fade away!

Here we go.

When people know the goal, assess where they are and connect the dots.

If people know where they are now, but either are begging for a miracle or are clueless about the next step, show them the next step and connect the dots.

And, finally, with everyone you coach or mentor, focus constantly on the process and on the keys to success.

I'm going to try not to be the problem anymore. Let's get into *Intervention*.

Chapter 2

Reverse Engineering My Brain:
Getting to Intervention

THIS WHOLE PROJECT BEGAN when someone asked, "How do you do it?"

One of my interns had been listening to me, week in and week out, on the phone with athletes.

"Do what?"

"Well, you seem to give solid advice every call and I recognize the basics we do, but, then..."

"What?"

"You seem to have some individual advice that just comes up out of your mouth, things that I've never heard you say, and it's like every call this happens."

Oh. Well, good question.

And it has taken me the better part of four years to answer it.

The short answer is, and really, this answers just about every question in the world of strength and conditioning, "It depends."

That's actually a pretty good answer, too. From my heart of hearts, I can tell you this: If someone prescribes a "one size fits all" approach to training, I can guarantee one thing: It's wrong. Many of us may fall in love with a new toy, a new fad, or a new idea that looks strangely like it was stolen from someone else, but sooner or later we find we're holding a bag of false promises…again. (I used to say a bag of doughnut holes, but then they came out with that product; I should get a kick-back.)

By way of an introduction, let's look at what I can offer. You have a fitness goal and ask if there's a strength training method or support program to assist in that goal. I think I have the skill-set to help you. By the time you finish reading this, you too will have the skill-set to help yourself and others.

Intervention is tool box of 10 questions and five principles. That's it.

Mixed into this system of questions and principles, I'll introduce you to some assessments I use, what I believe are the fundamental human movements, and the way I put all this together into a lifelong program. But the answers to these questions almost don't matter. Oh, I'm very fond of them! And it was 35 years of lifting, competing and coaching that lead me to these answers. But as long as you are asking the 10 questions and following these five principles, you will find Point A and you will get to Point B in the most direct route. If you skip a few questions and ignore a principle or two, you may still get there, but one of my athletes might be standing there asking what took you so long.

I take these questions seriously because for most of my career I have dealt with very serious athletes. Asking "what do you want" was an easy place to start and the 0.001% of athletes with truly elite goals were usually pretty serious when they told me, "I want to go to the Olympics." "I want the world record." "I want to play three more years in the NFL."

But then there's the other 99.999%. And therein lies the problem. As you go through *Intervention,* you are going to assume you have answers to the questions, but I challenge you have the courage to answer with honesty.

Let's start with my first rant. Nothing drives me crazier than when people whine, complain, bitch, manipulate and twist the world around to get what they want. And they get it. Then, it seems that wasn't what they wanted after all.

I have seen it in love and marriage, horse and carriage, and, of course, the fitness industry. Someone will ask to lose or gain something; we put together the greatest minds in the field to solve the issue, and we find that same someone a day later hung over and injured from an impromptu beer basketball game.

Later in this book I'm going to ask you the first question, "What do you want?"

Here's the thing: I'll believe you when you tell me!

And that's my problem. All too often, I've spent a great amount of time and energy coaching, writing, teaching and assisting someone to do something that really, at best, was a whim. I like women, I hate whims.

As the answer to "what do you want?" thuds around the air, I am also listening to very important clues to find out if this a goal I can help with. I ask many of the questions in the *Intervention* toolkit as a way to discover if you're talking to the right guy. Is it a health or a fitness question? If it's health, I apologize almost right away, because health, as Phil Maffetone explained, is the optimal interplay of the organs. If you choose not to wear a helmet and on a bet leap down a mountainside on some kind of high speed conveyance, I can only do so much. I'm a strength coach, not your mother.

However, if you have a fitness goal, I perk right up. If you really know what you want, and you have a fitness goal, a strength coach can almost universally help. But as we go through *Intervention*, I am also listening for how much I can help you. I am not your doctor and I am not your physical therapist. Many of the questions in our toolkit are dedicated to answering the question people ask the most: Can you help me, coach?

Well, of course, but, and you should be able to say this along with me: It depends.

Or so I thought for years. Now, I think the strength coach can have a very important role in helping you get your fitness goals. In some cases, the role will be very keen. But as I take you through *Intervention*, how much I can help will depend entirely on the courage you have in answering the 10 questions with honesty, and following the five principles with integrity.

These five principles I'm about to share with you are the most important coaching lessons I possess. I have learned these lessons the hard way every time I deviated from them. Let my stalls, sputters, dead-ends and surgeries be your lessons. It's cheaper and easier for you because I've gone ahead so blindly! Oh, I know most of you will try to turn a park bench into a bus bench, which I'll be sure to explain shortly. And that you'll all bite off more diet than you can chew. Your faith in the path will ebb and wane, but if you keep asking yourself the 10 questions and keep following the five principles, you'll find your way back.

I call this system *Intervention* because I've used it for years to teach people how to find Point A when they have gotten lost on the way to Point B. And honestly, it helps a lot of people figure out Point B, too. *Intervention* is how I make my money, but I wish people didn't have to use it. Oh, I know. If people never got lost and instead moved with Godspeed to their all their fitness goals, I would be broke! But I know from experience that no one stays on the path. Everyone gets lost. I'm teaching you *Intervention* because you and your clients will get lost and calling me is very expensive.

And while I hope you'll use it to complete your fitness journey, I also know there's a better way.

Before We Intervene: There's a better way to do this

There's a better way to do this than me being on the phone with a 26-year-old NFL defensive tackle telling him to do this or that. Ideally, we'd have a system where everyone would learn the basic movements and pattern training at an early age. As a child, I had physical education, and I was lucky: The instructor of my ninth-grade PE class taught me the basics of lifting and training. This had a major impact on why my high school was so successful in sports.

What kinds of things would we be teaching if we still had this education? In my little part of the world, we would teach these primary movements—

- ◆ Swing, Goblet Squat, Getup—the kettlebell foundation
- ◆ Military Press, Front Squat, Power Clean, Bench Press—barbell
- ◆ Hurdle Walkovers, Farmer Walks, Cartwheels, Forward Rolls, Tumbling, Shoulder Rolls

- General Movement and Mobility Work
- Later…Deadlift, Back Squat, Sled Work, Prowlers and Car Pushes

This is called systematic education. Systematic education takes the courage to start at the basic level each and every time when learning a new skill. It's obviously not for everyone, as the internet is filled with examples of people who have skipped ahead and woe to those who follow that lead. There's a crucial need to learn the basics, the step-by-step progression and the road to mastery. Failure to do so leads to issues later, from injury to worse. If you don't believe me, feel free to watch some internet videos of idiocy.

Sadly, few come to me with this background. *Intervention* begins with a few questions. Then I give a single recommendation or perhaps two, and wait a few weeks for the phone to ring. I pick it up and hear, "It was so simple; I should have thought of this myself!"

And I thank the fine person on the telephone for the insight and move back to the rest of my day.

To me, the system is simple. It's based on tools that allow me to get past the clutter and junk of the fitness industry and focus the athlete or non-athlete back on the goals. The tools clear away all of the this and thats of machines, straps, wraps, snaps, chains, balls and assorted voodoo that make training more complex than a trip to Mars. Most of it's junk, true, but what we want to do is focus on the tools that provide a leap of improvement.

Here's the problem: When we get to the end here, you'll shrug your shoulders and say how simple and obvious this all is. I know that. But, simple and obvious is what genius is all about.

Chapter 3

The 10 Questions

1. What is your goal? Meaning...*where's your point B!*
2. Is this a health or a fitness goal?
3. Will this goal allow you to spiral out, to enlarge your life?
4. What quadrant is your goal in?
5. How old are you?
6. What do you lift in the weightroom?
7. What are your gaps and are you willing to go back to the basics?
8. Let's just double-check a few things...assess, reassess, re-reassess.
9. The issues—Are you willing to correct your problems?
10. Would you mind if everything was seamless from start to finish?

So, these are the 10 questions. I'm going to call them tools, as these hold the answers that allow me to help you figure out the path. Some are like a GPS and others are more like the batteries that power the GPS. The first five are simple for anyone to answer, but require courage to deliver honest, useful answers. The second five take a bit more thought and work, but less courage.

What we have is a 10-question toolbox, followed by your answers. Then, the magic happens as I give you the answers to the answers!

The answers to the answers are these five principles.

1. Strength training for lean body mass and joint mobility work trump everything else.
2. Fundamental human movements are fundamental.
3. Standards and gaps must be constantly assessed.
4. The notion of park bench and bus bench workouts must be applied together throughout the training lifetime.
5. Constantly strive for mastery and grace.

But, let's not get too far ahead of ourselves. Like the King in *Alice in Wonderland* tells us…

> *"Begin at the beginning," the King said gravely,*
> *"and go on till you come to the end. Then stop."*

Coach Steve Ledbetter is an outstanding young coach who has taken the Intervention System and run with it. He outlined four of his clients for us, and his stories will give insights about applying Intervention to most people.

Coach Stevo's Case One

This client is the dream of most trainers. She's motivated and ready to work. But she's also lost. She doesn't know where she wants to go or even where she is. She's doesn't know Point A or Point B. Most personal training clients seek help from this place—lost and unaware.

It happened slowly. Not at first, of course; the first 10 pounds were obviously beer weight that happened at college. But all of her friends put on the same 10 pounds, so it didn't seem so bad. Anyway, she needed new work clothes. That excuse worked for almost five years, but after five more pounds, it was wearing as thin as the denim between her thighs. She joined a gym down the street from work and told herself she'd go every day because it was convenient. The gym also conveniently renewed her membership every January, so the hit to her Visa bill was an odd reminder that she had pedaled, ellipticaled and hip-hop danced yet another pound into her jeans since the previous January. Ten years as an adult, and she was 20 pounds from freshman orientation. She tried a diet here and there. She took some weightlifting classes. She did the right things, but year after year her fat jeans kept becoming just her jeans.

Until that boy on the subway said to her, "Move it, tubby."

Then slowly wasn't an option.

Motivation is for Navy SEALs and marathoners. She wasn't motivated after that subway ride; she was a fury of laser-focused rage. She filled the garbage can with ice cream, pretzels, and everything else with a carb in it. She bought a Nike Fuel Band, running shoes, a wireless scale for her bathroom and a nutritional scale for her kitchen.

And even after an hour of boot camp, she made the little red number on the elliptical go higher than she ever had seen it go. She didn't care that she was 30 minutes late for work; this would be her life now. Sweat and hunger meant she was making progress.

A week later, her new scale had a new number. It was lower, but not as low as the sweat and hunger suggested it would be. Every muscle ached and she wanted toast. How do people do this? How do people stay angry long enough lose the weight? How do people live without ice cream and nights out? She needed help, but she didn't even know what to ask for.

"Just tell me what to do. I don't know where I'm going, but I know I don't want to be here."

Chapter 4

First Question:
What's your goal?

YOU NEED TO ANSWER THIS. I can't do this for you. Think about it and find clarity. There are plenty of better authors out there—Earl Nightingale comes to mind—who do a better job on this than me.

This is going to be your Point B. My job, honestly, is to unpack your Point A, but help me out: Have an idea about where you want to go! I don't want to abandon you here because I know how much people struggle to find Point B, so here are a few things about this idea.

First, a few years ago, this whole "I need to be prepared for anything" macho stance started to dominate the internet. I recently read a funny line about how many college students know exactly what they are going to do if a Zombie Apocalypse happens, but have no idea about what to do after graduation. If you are preparing for anything, it's going to be hard to do. It's like what Stephen Wright said about having everything: Where would you put it?

Before "prepared for anything," the high intensity training guys who referred to themselves as HIT Jedi ruled the internet, so I like to think we've come a long way. The internet went from preaching "one set to failure" to "prepare for anything" in a very short period of time.

And, for most of us, both approaches are fraught with issues.

My issue, only recently clarified, is that this way of thinking, this prepare for anything, turns Point B into a circle. Well, the question of Point A still comes up, of course, but you'll notice even if you start right smack in the middle of a circle, any progress in any direction takes you in a direction away from your goal.

Even if your goal is "prepare for anything," trust me on this: If you get stronger, almost universally, you'll find the path to your goals is easier. So, get stronger first. After you're strong, you can prepare to fight a Great White shark with a spark plug or another kitchen utensil. Choose wisely!

Remember, these guys say to prepare for anything. This would be "anything." You should also be prepared to make a space ship out of dental floss too, I would imagine.

Which brings me to the shortest, but most important point ever.

Why strength training?

Good question.

The answer—Brett Jones once told me this—

"Absolute strength is the glass. Everything else is the liquid inside the glass. The bigger the glass, the more of everything else you can do."

Lifting weights is the quickest way to build strength. As your strength goes up, everything else can be expanded, too.

It's a simple point, so don't miss it!

Many elite fitness competition trainers believe that basic strength levels allow them to not train as hard in terms of time and apparent use of energy and still remain lean with less work than those who ignore strength.

The more I teach this point and listen to the excellent feedback, the more I hear real world examples about this.

Recently, a woman told me her friends can't make a mistake.

What? Well, what she told me was this: Since they were attacking fat loss with aerobic work and strict dieting, they didn't have any wiggle room. The woman, who holds herself nearly year-round at a very impressive 19% bodyfat, told me she enjoys desserts, cocktails, BBQs and fine food. But, and this is a big but, she can also do 10 pullups. She is very strong in the weightroom. In other words, her glass is so big, she can afford to cheat a little here and there.

That made no sense to me. Then I watched her train and thought about some other women I work with. When she presses an impressive kettlebell overhead (half her bodyweight with one hand!), her entire system has to gather up resources, and then adapt and recover from the effort. When little Edna at my gym thinks the five-pound dumbbell is heavy, she isn't going to tax her body very hard.

Edna can't eat cake.

It is almost a cliché now, but this leads us to another issue. I watch moms pick up, put down, lift, swing, load and carry fairly large loads all the time. We call these loads 'children.' Yet, when we get to the gym, we seem to think a woman needs to use very light loads. Like Milo and his calf, perhaps we should start women off with an eight-pound weight and progress upwards as the child grows.

One final point. There's a television commercial about a woman who falls and can't get up. She makes a famous statement I'm sure is copyrighted, but look, picking yourself off the ground or rolling yourself to a position so you can get up might save your life. You owe it to yourself and your loved ones to keep your strength up for as long as you can.

For many people, the most shocking thing they may ever read is this—

Get strong to get lean!

So as you are contemplating your goal, remember the glass. Do not just get strong for strong's sake! But you might find it valuable to ask yourself how many of your goals would be easier if you were working with a keg instead of a shot glass. And maybe it'll be a little easier to hold all the qualities you need to "prepare for anything" in something a little bigger than that schmedium t-shirt.

Finally, another unappreciated insight that comes up in this process is that *Intervention* also helps people with Point A. If you only hear one thing I preach about coaching, listen to this: It's not just assessing, but constant assessment. Most people lose track of where they are because they forget to assess. The laundry isn't shrinking your pants, the sizes of clothes aren't shrinking, and you can't get too comfortable with "having one more just this time" too often.

How do you assess where you are? Keep reading. But taking the time every now and then to reassess your Point B could be a good idea. As you get a little further down the path, it might be smart to look around and see if you like where you're headed.

Second Question:
Is this a health or a fitness goal?

AT FIRST, MOST PEOPLE who read the following brush it off like
a wisp of hair on a windy day. Do that at your peril.

> *Be sure you know whether your goal tilts*
> *towards the health side or the fitness side*
> *before you get too far along the path.*

Not long ago, a woman asked me about losing five pounds of
bodyweight. I was kind and courteous and told her she probably
wanted to lose five pounds of body fat, as losing five pounds of
bodyweight is easy: Chop off part of a limb.

My advice was safe and sane. It was the same basics I tell
everyone: Lower your carbs, add some fish oil, drink more water

and lift a few weights. It's not sexy, and it certainly isn't anything that gets the blood pumping. I admit it—I'm boring.

She signed up with a personal trainer who had one of those one-day certifications for about a thousand dollars and promised her "elite" training and used terms like "hard core" and "bad ass." Within a few months, she left her family, started dating the trainer and lost her house. Later, he dumped her and moved on to another gym girl. The good news? She lost the five pounds.

Knowing the difference between health and fitness goals may seem trivial, but confusing the two yields some pretty ludicrous decisions. What is this insanity I continue to see in the strength, conditioning and fitness world where people will trade their futures of chasing great-grandchildren around a park for a temporary fix on a bodypart? I can only help with part of the madness, but I am willing to step up here. Really, the bulk of my rantings, not only live, but online and in articles, centers around this lunatic idea that somehow putting yourself next to death's door is good for you. Oh, I know the T-shirts—

Pain is weakness leaving the body.
That which doesn't kill me makes me strong.

When did simple questions like, "I want to feel better; can you help me?" or "I would like to lose a few pounds; what should I do?" turn into battlefield tactics? I've never seen a T-shirt that said, "I want to walk to the mailbox on the day I die," but I am pretty sure more people would identify with that goal than an all-out war to get that 20th pullup. The issues of health, fitness and longevity impact every fitness goal and it's important to know the differences between these before you commit every available resource you have to that next pullup. I'm going to tell you—it's going to take a while, but let's get through the first issue now, the idea that health and fitness are the same. They're not and when you confuse them, you really start down the wrong road.

I've been using Phil Maffetone's definition of health for a long time—

Health is the optimal interplay of the organs.

Health is something that can always get a little better. Health is something measured by blood tests, longevity and the lack of bad health. Health is not illness. Tumors and high blood pressure and fainting are not signs of good health. Health is something we mostly take for granted until we don't have it.

In fact, I remind myself often to breathe deeply, smile and enjoy a moment of good health. It's a gift.

That isn't fitness? No.

Fitness is simply the ability to do a task.

Throwers are fit for the task of throwing. Jumpers are fit for the task of jumping and sprinters are fit for the task of sprinting. Years ago, a guy I know jumped into the shallow end of a swimming pool, drunk, and broke his neck. He can't move well, but he fathered two sons. He is fit for the task of procreation, although he can't walk. If you throw the discus 244 feet then need a nap for an hour and can't jog to catch the bus back the Olympic Village, you're the new world record-holder and no one is going to remember anything else about this story.

If you can do 100 pullups or run a marathon, but you have a major cancer lurking inside your body, you're fit for a task, but are not healthy. The issues are separate, but often impact each other down the line.

People often comment on the way I train athletes—my throwers throw. For the record, my jumpers jump and my sprinters sprint. I use this simple formula for many aspects of life.

Here's the thing: My throwers don't run. My throwers don't do agility or jumping or, really, just about anything besides throw and lift. Why? I want them to be fit to throw.

Our mantra is two-fold—

- Smooth goes far.
- Fit goes far.

"Fit for what?" is the correct follow-up question. The more a thrower throws, the smoother the technique and the farther the implement goes. The more a thrower throws, the fitter the thrower. Sure, your athlete might jog more than mine, but there's nothing in the rulebook that rewards jogging for throwers.

For health, I have my throwers floss their teeth twice day, I insist they wear seatbelts and helmets on bikes or motorcycles and encourage a generous use of fish oil. Moreover, I encourage my throwers to find a life partner willing to remain physically active, to optimize rest and recovery and discover a spiritual life. But jogging? Insane cardio workouts? Nope, that's an issue of fitness or for throwers, a lack thereof.

The following are the 10 rules I give everyone for health or fitness. The first eight are health-related, and the last two are universally true for any fitness goal.

1. Don't smoke.
2. Wear your seat belt, and use a helmet when appropriate, too.

3. Learn to fall…and recover!
4. Eat more protein.
5. Eat more fiber.
6. Drink more water.
7. Take fish oil capsules.
8. Floss your teeth. This is key for your heart health… look it up!
9. Keep your joints healthy.
10. Build some muscle.

Achieving clarity on the role of health and fitness was the single biggest hurdle in my coaching career. All too often, I, like almost everyone else in the field, tried to do this and that and this and that for myself and my athletes and found that we got ourselves not only farther and farther from our goals, but sick and injured, too. When you keep mixing up health and fitness, you'll find the two often run into each other down the road. You can only sacrifice health for fitness for so long and vice versa. The point is to know the compromises you are making and why.

Is it healthy to throw something with your right hand 10,000 times a year for 40 years? NO! But my fitness for the task of throwing the discus is what has made the rest of my career possible and allowed my children to go to college and for me to have Champagne Wednesday with my wife Tiffini. I am not saying your goal should be health over fitness, or even the other way around. But look at the answer you gave to question one, and give some serious thought to what kind of a goal you have. Is it health or fitness?

In addition, Robb Wolf noted we should also keep an eye on longevity, because it's probably not worth dying over a goal like winning the World's Thinnest Woman Prize, if they give one.

After I started to suffer some pretty serious (blinding, agonizing, terrifying) pain in my left hip, I knew I needed to give a lot of thought to longevity. I didn't know that soon enough, and competed in a few Highland Games with a femur made of oatmeal, but after a while I started to rethink how long I wanted to be fit to throw versus how long I wanted to be healthy.

Keep in mind that health and longevity are different than losing "this" around your midsection or running five miles at a fundraiser. It's when people mix up these two that the real issues appear.

Third Question:
Will this goal allow you to spiral out— to enlarge your life?

I THINK MY FIRST GLIMPSE into the art of lifelong fitness happened in the second grade (the best three years of my life). The fact that I remember a talk from the early 1960s, decades and miles ago, is enough to thank the memory of Sister Maria Assumpta and her few minutes at the chalkboard. Sister walked up to the board and chalked a basic compass shape. Rather than North, South, East and West, she replaced the sections with Work, Rest, Play and Pray. Very simple, she told us, your lives should always live in a balance with these four key aspects of life.

If you work too much, you ignore important things and, although the phrase was to be uttered years later in a different economic time, you burn out.

If you rest too much, you become slothful and ignore real living.

If you play too much, you'll be like the grasshopper from Aesop's tale and winter will be harsh. Sister never went into praying too much as she did have a religious vocation.

Pray can easily be alone time or an appreciation of goodness or beauty. I know of several moms who have come up to me after workshops to tell me their kids' lives were saved by having someone take them away to give Mom a few hours of quiet. There's something restful about just watching a waterfall or a plane land at night, too.

Breathe in and breathe out and enjoy it.

Like natural fractals, those objects that seem to display a self-repeating structure when looked at from a great distance or up close—think snowflakes, mountains, rivers, broccoli and the blood system—one's life from birth to death can be looked at by this balance compass.

As a first step, look back over your life and find times where you seemed whole and your life was full. Usually you'll realize you were holding work, rest, play and pray in balance. You took care of business, but also took your shoes off and played in the sand. You probably had good friends, worthy of the name, and some time alone to take care of your personal and spiritual needs.

Narrowing this down from the fractals model—and if you don't remember where you learned fractals, think about *Jurassic Park*—can give you some insights about how these four compass points can illuminate a successful venture. One's day, one's workout and perhaps even one's morning coffee could be seen this same way.

Let's use a training day.

Too much working out can lead to soreness, injuries and fatigue. What's worse is that the workouts that work you out (literally) tend to only be short-term, yet burn one out for the long haul (life!).

Too much rest in a workout can be fairly broad. I've had people ask for all kinds of help, and then in responding, I discover the person never actually trains. Or I see a person who may have to warm up again to deal with the excessive rest time. Few people honestly have a lack-of-rest issue in training. They tend to rest, sit, sleep and watch TV so much that their rest reserve is well in hand.

Too much play is something we don't see much anymore either. I'm convinced most of us would never need workout DVDs or personal trainers if we just met in the field after work and played some games. The game of tag is an under-realized workout. Now it's possible to have too much socializing during a workout. A lot of gym rats, and I am as bad as anyone, would rather talk about great workouts than to have one!

Too much alone time is something I've had to undo in my training. I trained in my garage for years, but found a lot was missing. Inviting friends over or popping by a gym every so often really helps me push myself harder than training alone. It's a small thing, but it makes a real difference in intensity.

So, the answer to all of this is to insist that you take some time and energy to think about how to balance a workout.

I recently learned this lesson again. I went to a workshop and was exposed to some very insightful new technical ideas on traditional movements like the windmill and the bent press. Everyone seemed willing to help, so much so that with this bit of advice and that bit of help, I became locked up. My brain was on overdrive.

Later, when I went home and only had one voice in my head (hold the jokes for later), I could use all the advice I was given, but one piece at a time. I needed both the camaraderie of the group and the intensity of the work to learn the movements, but I needed some quiet time alone to master them. It's a point worthy of consideration. I discovered this small insight about the way I learn, and many people have told me the same is true for them: I need both community and solitude to master a movement or a concept.

This might be the brilliance of homework for students. An honest attempt at working out a geometry proof can allow the flash of insight later in the classroom during a review. This is why many people get good ideas in the shower or driving around in a car or bicycle. Once that interior noise abates a bit, the answer or the clarity seems to rise.

I decided years ago to consciously harvest this skill in my life. It is worth your time to make to fill in the following chart.

	Work	Rest	Pray	Play
Health				
Fitness				
Longevity				

Robb Wolf mentioned that I should add longevity to the life balance compass. As early as you can in life, it's worth thinking about living as well as you can, as long as you can. When considering something that may be unsafe, unhealthy or dangerous, at least take a second to toss it through the longevity equation. Sure, petting a Great White might be your idea of an epic moment, but consider a shark cage.

Note that I include performance in the worksheet. For whatever reason, no matter how many times I define fitness, most people still don't hear "the ability to do a task." I added performance to the table, and now many people seem to hear that as completing a marathon or going dancing again.

Although any unit of time will work—lifetime, decade, year, month, week, day or hour—think a bit globally on the chart the first time you ponder it. Let's use the next year on your first attempt. In each area, add a short note about how you'll use your full mind, body and spirit to engage all four points and all three pillars (Robb's term) to balance yourself this next year.

For example—

Work

Health

I will keep a supply of dental floss, fish oil capsules and water at work. I'll also lift weights twice a week.

Fitness/Performance

I'll finish the 5K Walk for Life.

Longevity

I will walk or bike or swim at least five days a week. Since the store is only a mile, I'll do all single-item shopping on foot.

Rest

Health

I will turn off the television at nine every evening unless there's a show I must see. Otherwise, I'll spend the time from nine to ten every night preparing for sleep.

Fitness/Performance

I will stand up from my desk every half an hour, and walk around for a few minutes to relax and recharge.

Longevity

Either through audiotapes, DVDs or lessons, I will learn to put myself into a relaxed, meditative state, and will do this several days a week.

Play

Health

I'll learn to laugh more at work. I will post Dilbert *and* Calvin and Hobbes *comic strips as appropriate to situations that arise. I'll laugh every day. I'm going to put comedy CDs in the car for the commute.*

Fitness/Performance

I'm going to say 'yes' to every chance to play in a game, no matter what the game.

Longevity

I will add at least one gathering a month to my schedule to just hang and graze with friends.

Pray

Health

I'll take some time each day to be alone for a few minutes.

Fitness/Performance

I am going to master [fill in a difficult task: the splits, a pistol, another lift, a yoga move]. Mastery is a path, not a goal, but get on the path.

Longevity

People who go to church live longer. I should consider where I am with this.

The key here is the next step—looking at all these 'I wills' and looking at the connections.

For this example, and it's just an example, the stress of the workplace is obviously a factor, as is time. Little things like less television and changing the commute into what many call 'the mobile university' might make a huge difference. Everybody has the same amount of time in a day, a week and a year, but how each of us spends it is a different thing.

Generally, making a small change for the better in one area of your life, something as simple as having floss sticks in your car and desk (yes, I keep repeating it), seems to carry over into the other areas. Once you start flossing, you seem more in tune with other things you put in your mouth and maybe you'll skip that birthday cake at the office party. Skipping the cake often gives you the courage to get home and get a little workout. Working out invigorates you enough to not slump into the couch and click on the TV.

Yes, it's that simple and yes, it works that well. When you have things dialed in, you'll probably laugh at the simplicity of our little chart. It's when you struggle that you need to wake up and reassess this focused attempt to have balance in your life.

What if You're Spinning Out of Balance?

RECENTLY AT A WORKSHOP by Dr. Paul Hammer, I saw an interesting way to spread the concept of health and fitness across a continuum. I love continuums and, well, in total candor…just get used to it.

The health and fitness continuum, if you will, starts on the far left with a green light. Imagine the standard traffic light to understand the point here. Green is go, yellow suggests caution and red means stop. As we move across this continuum, we move from green to yellow to red.

If you're on the green side of the continuum, congratulations, you have things dialed in. My goal is to be in the green area for every area of my life.

- My relationships with my family are fine.
- There is no real insanity in our financial areas.
- I have time to help out in the community.
- I'm enjoying life, keeping in decent shape and sleeping well.

For me, life in the green side is all about having some reserves. I have enough in the bank to cover a minor tragedy of life, like a broken water heater, and I have enough time to help a buddy move a couch. I have enough energy to train and enough energy after I train to still enjoy some entertainment with my family. In other words, in green nobody puts an arm around you and says, "Hey, I'm a little worried about this or that."

And by the way, if there's nobody in your life to warn you about excess, it's a sign you aren't in green.

Yellow—caution of course—is not as bad as you may think, but it's important to remember caution from driver's education class. This is not time to speed up!

In some of the most productive times of my life, I've also felt myself spinning out of balance. At these times, I often just look at the calendar. If there's relief in sight, I don't worry too much.

A while back, I had this week—

> **Friday and Saturday:** State track meet, where I was the head coach and my daughter won the state championship in the shot put
>
> **Sunday:** Packing a household for our move across several states

Monday: Full day of work *and* finishing finals for my online courses

Tuesday: Full day of work *and* Baccalaureate for my daughter—I'm a teacher so I had to be there early

Wednesday: Track and Field Banquet—as head coach I had to organize and run it

Thursday and Friday: Packing

Saturday: Graduation and graduation parties

Sunday: Graduation party for my daughter

Monday: Movers show up to move us—Tiff and I drive to California, leaving our daughters behind

Basically, in one week I had enough work and labor and pressure and emotions to fill several years. This was a yellow light time, but I knew I had at least two quiet weeks after unpacking before anything else came up. Knowing the pressure would ease eased the pressure. I was lucky in that I had friends, family, community and a schedule that supported this stressful time.

I really had to work hard to be so lucky.

Red lights mean fate has other plans for you at the moment. That's something like a DUI, an arrest, a serious injury or other traumatic issues. This is not the area of friendly assistance. This is a time for professional help.

Like the old joke about knowing you're going to have a bad day at the office when you see the *60 Minutes* crew in the waiting room, a red light stage is a bad day. It's far beyond the scope of this book to discuss these issues, but if you find yourself in the yellow light situation long enough, address it now! Don't wait for the red light.

But don't focus on the negative here. The great insight I came across in the mid-1990s about the life balance compass is that these four great truths of work, rest, play and pray tend to spiral out. If I decide to work harder, I find it natural now to increase my play. I play harder when I work harder. My vacations, perhaps reflecting the increase in money from working harder, are bigger. I find there's a tremendous synergy when I look at consciously increasing my other compass points when I take on a task.

There is a wonderful chapter in *Parkinson's Law* about asking a busy man to write a letter. It will be done in a minute. The author, C. Northcote Parkinson, contrasts this with someone who has almost nothing to do, and this person sweats over what kind of envelope to use. Busy people tend to get more things done. If you look for ways to expand yourself in all four directions, you'll get more things accomplished. The more you do, the more you do.

Becoming more balanced also begins to affect how you go about attaining your goals. I became famous for hosting very hard workouts in my backyard along the river. We've had over two dozen people show up, but around 10 or so is the typical number. We have all kinds of equipment and gear and we take turns pulling and tugging and sprinting and running and carrying various odds and ends.

It's a fun, playful workout and we keep the grill going the whole time. After training hard, we hang on the deck and graze for hours, laughing and enjoying life. Of course, I balance this with easy workouts where I train alone and try to figure ways of besting my friends and thinking of even more devious ways to exhaust them when they come back.

Let me add this for clarity. There are two tools stuck into one here. First, you need to look at the spiral. If you're going to do more work, you need to actively look at your play, pray and rest areas. If you don't expand those, which wonderfully also expand work in a synergistic way, you're planning failure.

The red, yellow and green light system provides a basic tool to decide "maybe not now!"

The impact on training is obvious. You can increase your work when you're in green. Red and yellow situations do not mean toss out your training, exercise or supplement regime. In fact, this is probably the time when a workout might be supportive of your other issues. It's not, however, the time to ratchet up the volume, intensity or load.

I'm working on teaching people to be more proactive about this so they can focus certain periods of the year on the reality of life. For example, a tax accountant would perhaps calendar out March and April as obvious yellow-light months. A teacher could do the same May and June and August and September. Certainly, it wouldn't be a bad idea for parents of younger children to put an "X" through December with all the concerts, pageants, plays and stuff.

During these times, certainly you should still train. But you need to focus more on another kind of training I call bus bench and park bench workouts. I'll go into great detail about what this means, but simply—

Bus Bench Workouts
When expecting results on time—like you're hoping the bus will be

Park Bench Workouts
An opportunity to explore and enjoy where you are in training

I realize this goes against the grain we see in most TV ads, internet chest pounding and monthly magazines. But, I don't have a chef, handlers, driver and full-time photoshopper. I just have me and that spreads me out a bit. I can't train like someone either paid to train or paid to look good.

Oh, and yes, this is contrary to what most people think. There's this idea that constant, exhaustive training is the only path to a goal. It's not true and it's destroying many people's journey toward their goals.

Chapter **8**

Fourth Question:
Which quadrant is your goal in?

THE CONCEPT OF QUADRANTS first appeared in my *Intervention* DVD, an introductory companion piece to this book, and shortly thereafter, in my book with Pavel, *Easy Strength*. I am proud of this contribution to the world of fitness and strength.

Like most coaches, I have been juggling the ever-expanding world of strength training with my sports athletes since I first blew my first whistle. Back in the 1970s, every month brought a new wave of magazines with new tools, programs and movements all guaranteed to change the lives of athletes. We could test a few, laugh at couple and generally keep one or two ideas from all the pulp. Today, through the internet we can literally get a new idea a minute. With the explosion of DVD programs and home training equipment that were claimed to be invented by a Navy SEAL or used by NFL players, most of us are swamped with piles of clutter.

A few years ago, the question came up, "What is the role of the strength coach?" Well, it is like the role of an English teacher; the answer is in the adjective.

Teach English.

Coach strength.

Then Pavel asked the follow-up question: *Yes, but what is the* **impact** *of the strength coach?*

This began a two-year process of trying to answer this question. I was worried the best answer I'd come up with would be, "It depends."

Finally, I worked out a simple four-part quadrant grid. These quadrants are based on two continuums—

- The number of qualities an athlete must have to excel at a sport
- How good the athlete needs to be at each of the those qualities relative to how good any athlete can be at that quality

Based on where these lines intersect, we split the impact of the strength coach into four quadrants. Having the ability to categorize a person in Quadrant Three instead of Quadrant Four allows us to discern what to add to a training program and, more importantly, what to ignore.

Quadrant One	Quadrant Three
Physical education class—*lots of low-level qualities*	Most people—*few qualities, at low level*
Quadrant Two	Quadrant Four
Collision sports, certain occupations—*lots of high-level qualities*	Rare athletic competition—*few qualities, at the highest level*

Quadrant One

The person in this quadrant is learning a lot of qualities at a low level, like a high school physical education class. Most people only get one shot in life for this quadrant. This is why the importance of a quality PE program can't be overemphasized. Here we learn the rules, the skills and the appreciation of games, sports and movement.

Quadrant Two

This quadrant houses the collision sports and occupations. A lot of qualities are needed, and the level of these qualities is quite high...amazingly high. This is football, rugby and Special Forces work. Sadly, most people plan to train in this quadrant, yet few actually *should* train in this manner.

Quadrant Three

This will sound odd, but here there's a need for few qualities at a low level. Most people fit in quadrant three, but elite athletes are most often found here, too. An elite track athlete needs technique and strength. The strength levels are amazing, but not high when compared to someone who just lifts like an elite Olympic lifter. In this quadrant a person may need the absolute strength to deadlift 600 pounds. That's a pretty big number, but let's remember the world record is approaching twice that. In Quadrant Three, it's all relative.

Quadrant Four

Here in quadrant four, we find the rarest of athletes. These are people who need very few qualities, but at the highest levels of human performance. Think 100-meter sprinters and Olympic lifters. Unless you are thinking of deadlifting 1,000 pounds or sprinting a 9.8 100-meter, you might not be here.

Life and Living in the Quadrants

Almost universally, when I help people through the *Intervention* program, I tell them they're in Quadrant Three. It's not laziness, it's reality. Sure, an NFL player *was* in Quadrant Two, but as a career moves on, training simplifies.

In fact, part of my "sad, but true" for nearly everyone I walk through this *Intervention* program is this: You are not in high school or college anymore!

And, that's probably a good thing. It's time to work on the two big things: hypertrophy—lean body mass increases, less fat and more muscle—and joint mobility.

Listen to me: Unless you bought this book with money you earned from breaking the world record in the 100 meters or for sacking an NFL quarterback, you *are* in quadrant three. And, that means the role of strength training will be in a yin and yang relationship with the meat of your goal (diet, for example, for fat loss or walking for general health, or throwing for a discus thrower).

The qualities I can impact as a strength coach are balanced with the one or two other qualities you need to develop. You need to learn to manage your options.

Sometimes I worry when I read a new article or pop into a workshop or clinic. I start to get excited about this new toy or idea. This goes through my mind—

"Yes, I can."

I have the resources. I went to the class. I sat through the clinic. I read the book. I can do it. That's right, with just a little information, I can add something new and pretty to a training program and sports system. My athletes ask, "Um, Coach, what about this other stuff we've been doing? Are we still going to do it?"

I don't know. I have a shiny new toy!

And, really, this is the problem. In Quadrant Two, everything probably works. I have made my career insisting that "everything works" and suddenly I become "the guy who worries that everything works."

Now, before you abandon me due to my lack of commitment, let me defend myself.

This is the problem with Quadrant Two activities like the collision sports and collision occupations: Everything only "probably" works. A football game, for example, is such a complex system that trying to assess what goes right and what goes wrong is, at best, guesswork. The very nature of Quadrant Two, with the sheer volume of qualities and the high level of these qualities necessary just to show up, makes it tough to see whether or not a new idea, plan, supplement, program or concept is really making a difference.

Here is the rub: Your competition may have started doing this new thing you have your eye on, so you need to ask some tough questions. If my opponents are adding this and that, do I need to add this or that? Or do I have a different situation and a different vision, so I don't need to add anything at this time? Or maybe—and this is often the case—this new idea is idiotic and I can save a lot of time and energy ignoring it.

The first thing that amazes people when they visit a Division One or professional sports team training facility is that they see, well, everything! Machines, kettlebells, med balls, ropes, climbers, rowing machines, cross-country ski machines…and I can go on and on. To recruit high school kids, one university coach told me they invested in a $25,000 machine they never use; it simply looked like something that would make you better.

Why? Why do these programs invest so much into strongman gear and Olympic bars, then never use them after the first week?

The answer is usually "everybody else is doing it." To keep up, we need to add this and that and this. Does it work? Well, who would ever know, because two months later we order the next newest, brightest toy in the store!

Quadrant Two, then, demands a special kind of thinking—managing compromises.

Managing Compromises Versus Managing Options
Managing Compromises

We can do anything, and it may or may not work. Or we can cut anything and it may or may not work. But, listen to this: If we spend a lot of time on this great new idea, how do we keep doing what got us here? And what if that idea really *is* the best thing since sliced bread? Welcome to compromises.

Let's talk.

It never fails that when the Super Bowl is on, someone will tell me that all Team X needs to do is "something like this" or "this play we used to do." It's laughable, of course, as the NFL teams run so many things that I can guarantee Old 97, the play that won the 1926 Rose Bowl is going to be in the playbook somewhere. Every idea the head coach, assistant coach, and offensive coordinator has had or heard of since they played the game in high school is probably in that playbook.

What most fans don't realize is that football teams can't go from this fun thing to that new idea very quickly. Printing plays in a book is cheap. Actually teaching those plays to a team with a finite memory for plays and systems is riskier. A 320-pound offensive lineman who all year was told to take three powerful steps forward, but now is told to go three steps back could end up in the place he started!

A counter to this stalemate we hear when working with collision sports and occupations is, "we gotta get back to (fill in the blank)." What happens as you flow through this or that new idea is pretty soon you feel like you're doing all these things, but you gaze back and see you've forgotten the basics that brought the success in the first place. The phrase in football is "you dance with the girl who brung ya."

But then you have to be wary of the other extreme of managing compromises. It's possible to throw the baby out with the bathwater when you decide (from the Latin root *dēcidere,* meaning "to cut or to kill") to forcefully shift directions.

Years ago, the football staff I was on ran a great offense called the Run and Shoot. I loved it. It had teams scrambling around trying to stop everything. We found that towards the end of each first half, we scored a fairly easy touchdown. The reason I thought this worked is that our offense stopped the clock a lot. Our team was used to being on the field about 20 minutes longer than the opposition was accustomed to. And I had evidence, because the number of plays were clearly higher when teams played us.

The following season, after long discussions about teaching and clarity, we decided to simplify and only do the Run and Shoot. As a coach, it was great: I had the whole offense in quicker and smoother with just one half of what we used to teach.

The catch was, we also started losing…a lot. When we simplified our offense, we cut this older, simpler offense based on "punch you in the mouth" plays called Blasts and Powers from the I Formation. During halftime in the previous season, the opposing coaches were remapping and redesigning their defenses for the Run and Shoot, so we came out in the I Formation and scored quickly against a confused defense. When we cut the I Formation, we also gave up a lot of winning because it was easier to defend and challenge the one face of our offense. The compromise for that simpler offense was losing, and that's a terrible compromise!

Welcome to the challenge of managing compromises. You can get too cute and get so back to the basics that you simplify yourself out of a job. Quadrant Two is not easy! But, this is why NFL coaches are paid so well. It's not an eight-hour day at that level.

So, how do you do it? How do you hold faithful to the basics, the givens, the core or the mission, and still try new things your competition is mastering while you wait to implement it? How do you manage the compromises?

First, as a strength coach this will always be about establishing the highest level of absolute strength we can. A team of athletes who are all at a relatively solid strength level trumps a program with super stars in the weightroom mixed with people who can't lift their own socks off the ground. The Big Blue Club for our high school boys and Big Silver Club for the girls were based on this insight.

Big Blue Club
>*Power Clean 205*
>*Deadlift 315*
>*Back Squat 255*
>*Front Squat 205*
>*Standing Press 115*
>*One-Arm Bench 32kg, 5 right, 5 left*
>*Power Clean & Jerk 165*

Big Silver Club
>*Power Clean 95*
>*Deadlift 205*
>*Back Squat 135*
>*Front Squat 95*
>*Standing Press 70*
>*One-Arm Bench 12kg, 10 right, 10 left*
>*Power Clean & Jerk 75*

Second, the strength and conditioning side needs to align with the overall program's vision. I often tell high school coaches that off-season training absolutely depends on the vision of the head coach. If your program is based on high speed and lots of running, your off-season training is track practice. Your people should be sprinting and hurdling. If your vision of football is based on smash mouth, hard-nosed contact, sleds and prowlers need to be a huge part of the off-season. Marry the ideas of the team philosophy and your weightroom vision.

Third, evaluate and assess your system. I know we all do this, but there has to be a real vision here. One can't win over time without a real vision of what is crucial. John Wooden's books and the work of a few others would be worth your time and investment.

Fourth, because Quadrant Two exists at such a rare air, these athletes need to be guided and supported by an overall challenge of excellence. I am an avid reader of all of Bill Walsh's work and I discovered that winning is a byproduct of standards of excellence. You can't have lousy care of game uniforms and obscene toilet facilities and call yourself a first-class organization. Success in Quadrant Two is going to come from excellence at every single thing we do.

Finally, and fundamentally, the art of managing compromises demands an ability to keep looking at the mission and goal while sifting through various new ways of achieving the mission and the goal. The key is, of course, remembering the two mantras of life.

The mission is to keep the mission, the mission.
The goal is to keep the goal, the goal.

Quadrant Three—Where Most of Us Live

Managing Options

The problem with the quadrants grid is the interesting fact that nearly everyone thinks they are elite, collision-living quadrant twos. How do I know this? By far, the most common question I answer is, "Am I in Quadrant Two?"

These are questions from people who want to learn the Olympic lifts, but only do them once every two weeks and the other 13 days are filled with cardio-busting workouts, bodybuilding and circuit training. Trust me, putting the bar overhead with 400 is *nothing* like doing 95 pounds for 50reps. I know, if you do the math (!!!), you will find that 400 for one is only 400 pounds of total work and 95 for 50 is like, well, a lot more, but, somehow, 400 still feels heavier.

I get email messages from people who want to lose some fat but spend time doing leaps onto boxes. I just don't get that.

But then, I also get messages from people who watch a one-minute clip from my DVDs on *Youtube* and ask if I can just send the rest to them. I always wonder if they want me to cook and clean for them, too, because they think I am their mother.

Here, however, is the inescapable truth—

> *Most of us move from Quadrant One*
> *to Quadrant Three and stay there.*

Sure, like me, you may have played a few years of football, Quadrant Two, but the bulk of life is spent here in Quadrant Three.

It's my fault Quadrant Three is thought to be feeble. I often joke that in Quadrant Three "we don't do much and we don't do it very well."

But I love Quadrant Three! I embrace it. Really, I love it. The greatest moment of clarity in my life came a few years ago when I had two full-time jobs—high school teacher and college instructor—two little girls at home, Kelly and Lindsay, and a wife always on the road. When I discovered at best all I could squeeze in was an hour of training each day, my lifting career exploded. Oddly, it is the same advice I gave my athletes, but there is no way I can possibly hear my own sound advice.

When you only have an hour to train, you have an opportunity to scrape away the excess and decide (remember, from the Latin root "to cut") what is important to you. This is life-changing, and in my case was a life-illuminating moment. When I went through this exercise, I discovered that life in Quadrant Three is not about managing compromises. I was not in Quadrant Two trying to decide which of the hundreds of athletic qualities I should favor in order to gain a competitive advantage.

My life was not that complex. I only needed a handful of qualities to excel in my sport. My life was simple and I needed balance.

Quadrant Three is a wonderful place where balance means more than in any other quadrant. And this is where the confusion comes in. I use the yin and yang symbol to explain the dynamic relationship between the role of absolute strength and technical mastery, but this symbol is not perfect because it misses the dynamic nature of this relationship.

There is strength and technique. But it's not 50/50 and the relationship is not static. Like a baby, you can't unlink the DNA from the father or the mother. The genes are so integral that the child is truly 100/100 percent of each parent.

With Quadrant Three athletes, you must understand this: Technical work is strength work; strength is technical. The two qualities flow into and build on each other. Mastery in the weightroom carries over to the ring, which brings knowledge that carries back into the weightroom and then back out to the ring. A strong person you teach to throw the discus or a good thrower you make strong will never throw as far as the thrower who seeks to master both aspects as complements to the other.

This dynamic balance is why I love Quadrant Three.

For a fat loss client, the same holds true: The diet or food program must be linked tightly to the exercise program. (I argue strength here, of course.) In the same way, the strength program should inform the diet.

A good personal trainer should spend as much time reviewing the food journal as it takes for the client to learn that the food journal is the essential key to success. Without the food journal and the peek into the reality of the week ahead, training is a half-way measure. The food journal informs the training; the training will impact the food journal, and mastery of the two will lead to a lifetime of easy weight management.

The longer I spend in this game, the more I realize that Quadrant Three is not an "either…or" proposition. Oh, certainly, we know people who move from fad diet to fad diet and get some improvements. But the improvements rarely stick. And, we all know the modern cliché, you can't outrun a bagel/doughnut/twinkie/whatever.

It has to be "both…and."

The problem with the strength, conditioning and fitness community today is that we have all fallen in love with the videos of NFL guys or ultimate fighters doing this and that and this in prepping for something. And I understand the appeal. Quadrant Two athletes are truly amazing spectacles of mastery and grace. Sometimes even I want to be that guy.

For most of us who are trying to scrub a few pounds of fat that has frowned over the belt or compete in a sport with a just a few qualities, we can get caught up in all of this fantastic stuff. And that's the problem. As I have noted endlessly: "Everything works…for about six weeks!"

Then what?

One of my favorite articles sheds a light on how we can quickly go from simple to complex—

"Brian Oldfield, Al Feuerbach, Bruce Wilhelm and Sam Walker favored the quick lifts, while George Woods and Randy Matson leaned toward the strength lifts. … If there was any real consensus among the champion shot-putters, it was that a mixture of quick and strength lifts is effective." ~Dave Davis, *Track Technique,* March and June 1974

The formula for success with these shot-putters is fairly simple, but you rarely see this recipe today. Here is the issue for any athlete, and in a moment I will expand this out to most people: One can achieve the highest levels of strength for throwing or sprinting or whatever through several routes.

These include—
Olympic lifting
Powerlifting
Strongman Training
Highland Games
Power Bodybuilding

Frankly, they all work. I'm sure blending these plans somehow would work better than just doing one, but that would be a tough experiment and probably would involve a time machine like the one I'm working on.

We can all agree that the quality the shot-putter needs is absolute strength. And now you see, these schools of strength training Davis was referring to are simply options. If there's a key to understanding Quadrant Three, it is these two words: Everything works.

Chapter 10

Everything Works

IT ALL WORKS. The goal of a thrower's strength and conditioning coach is to simply get the thrower stronger. As I have offered on countless occasions, there is no simpler quality to improve than strength: You just lift weights.

Technical, tactical and flexibility issues, if needed for performance, may take a few years to develop, but I can make you stronger for your sport and probably impact performance in three to six weeks. That is lightning in the sports world, and this is why every single sport has lifting weights as an essential part of basic training. Sure, you can find someone who didn't a decade ago, but that is rare air today.

It's all about managing options. Everything works. Remember that, embrace that, cherish that and keep "Everything Works" written on the wall of your gym, weightroom or dojo. Just remember, too, that it only works for about six weeks.

Reading Tommy Kono's outstanding books, I was reminded time and again about how he embraces both bodybuilding and Olympic lifting. Tommy settled on an eight-week build up to a lifting meet, then back in the gym to bodybuild and refresh himself. I think if it works for the greatest lifter in history and Mr. Universe—Tommy won Olympic gold medals as well as Mr. Universe—it might be worth considering. Tommy Kono was and is the master of managing options.

Fat loss, too, is a Quadrant Three goal. Again, it comes down to managing options. What diet works? They all work! It's about sticking to one. I have done well on Meat, Leaves and Berries, Atkins, the Velocity Diet, the Slow Carb Diet and the Eades' diet of three protein shakes and one-meal-a-day plan. The best diet I ever did was the F-Plan Diet when I consumed massive amounts of fiber each day. Oh, I got bloated and my joints ached, but I got plenty of exercise sprinting to the toilet.

Folks, diets and ways of eating are all about options. The actual dietary approach doesn't matter. Really, who cares what you are going to eat; what got you fat is what you ate!

Adherence trumps dogma in dietary disciplines. We also know this is true on the strength side: A bad program consistently administered trumps a perfect program (if one ever existed) done with lack of vigor. I'm convinced, by the way, that this is part of the secret that every program works for about six weeks: One's early dedication makes the craziest of ideas work.

Like I tell people who don't listen to my sane advice: Fine. I will be here next year, too, and we can follow up on this after your surgeries.

On the other side of the fat loss coin, really, again—everything works and it always has. Whatever you write down, whether it is African Disco Dance or Step Marching Spandex or Kettlebell Swings, it will work. The problem is a little odd: As you become more and more efficient, you get less and less benefit. A modern dance class will just about kill me as every time the class does Step-Ball-Change, I will have done 20 extra moves. Oh, it will be fat loss for me, but our little darling Twinkle Toes to my right had better have a perfect diet, because she is just going through the paces.

Exercise for fat loss needs to be as inefficient as possible. That is why I like the swing: You expend tons of energy and go nowhere! But, and many disagree with me here, as you get better and better at swings, these too can become too efficient. If you go from 75 to 2,000 swings a workout and stop losing fat, you may need to look for alternatives, additions or another bell.

Fat loss is about managing options. Pick a diet and follow it. Find a fitness program and follow it. Take notes, keep a food journal and do your due diligence on your before-and-after photos, your measurements and your skin-fold tests. Yes, the diet on the cover of the weekly magazine *is* better than what you're doing, and so too is the new DVD you saw on TV. It might not be true, but isn't this how we think?

All I am asking is that you stick with your plan long enough to evaluate it honestly. That might take a few weeks, but the effort you expend on mastering the basics of food and exercise will pay dividends in the long run.

If you are a Quadrant Three athlete, yes, a resounding yes, you have options. On the technical side, you can jump and throw with a variety of methods. I just read a fascinating piece by a British long jumper, Chris Tomlinson, who said he uses the "hang" method, the most basic and primitive method of long jumping, because it's simple and holds up under the stress of competition. He can focus on attacking the board, not his flight (and, according to physics, he has this right): "I prefer to use a style where as little can go wrong as possible in the jump."

Maybe you pick this method over that, and that's fine with me. Now, master it. Get a little strong, improve your technique and you should do better. But stick with the options you choose for long enough to master them!

The hardest part of Quadrant Three is not getting caught up in all the options of this wonderful buffet of diets and training programs. Have the courage to pick one and see where it takes you. Finish what you start. As the ancients taught us—

- Plan the Hunt.
- Hunt the Hunt.
- Discuss the Hunt. (See J. Stanton's *The Gnolls Credo* for details)

Keep it in that order. When you diet or train, you are in the hunt. You need to save all the thinking and talking for another time. But with all the options available at the buffet and all the different people and stimuli vying for your focus, it's no wonder so many of us fail at managing options and fail at keeping the goal the goal.

Throughout my career, I have fallen back on three tools every coach and trainer—and parent and teacher—could use for every situation and setting.

They are—

Checklists
Rituals
Deliberate practice

Checklists

If I could tell you one secret to success, it would be making checklists. I'm not sure how I first came across them, but I know I was developing them in the mid-1990s. Paul Northway, the great Judge Memorial Catholic High School discus thrower, had a laminated checklist for meets. As I recall, he wrote—

+ Discus
+ Shoes
+ Towel
+ Jacket
+ Water
+ Sunscreen
+ Snack Food
+ Money
+ Sunglasses

Over time, we added more items, including a measuring tape as many high school track meets in Utah are so bad there wasn't always a tape for the discus.

Eventually, the list included practically everything we could forget. Here is the key: When we do the same thing more and more often, we're going to slip on the basics.

When I run a workshop, I send the host a checklist that includes the little things. Nametags are almost universally the most overlooked item, because we worry about flights, meals and hotels, things that can be taken care of months ahead, and miss the tiny packet of nametags that will simplify my life for the entire workshop.

Checklists keep your brain from focusing on a bunch of stuff and make you think about what's important, like Lou Holtz' famous WIN formula: What's Important Now. Nothing on the checklist will be that important when you remember it, but forgetting any one item might put us in a difficult position. What's Important Now could be "where are my shorts?" versus "let's run this race."

The very act of making a checklist demands that you—

+ Tell me everything you need.
+ Tell me what's really important.

The longer you are in any game or job, the more and more you will clump these checklist items. The first time you make pancakes, you read the recipe. The 20th time, you don't read the recipe, but forget the egg (or whatever). The 100th time, you breeze over the recipe clumping together the various steps, but you still check the recipe!

It all comes down to something I call etching. Etching is the term used for drawing on glass and I love the image for training… and life, too. Etching is doing something over and over, making all the excess fluff unimportant. You can see proper etching when the best athletes move seemingly without effort.

Checklists allow you to etch. You are saying "This is important."

That's why I often talk about menus for a family and chore lists for everyone in the community. My wife Tiffini and I adopted these techniques years ago. I made little cards and put them on the wall and in my cubby at work. For example—

Monday
Dinner: steak, salad
Chore: white laundry and walk-through (everyone walks around the shared living areas and puts away books, shoes, jackets and junk)

Tuesday
Dinner: Viking enchiladas
Chore: dark laundry and walk-through

Wednesday
Dinner: jambalaya
Chore: clean bathrooms and walk-through

I have discussed this in the past, but people miss the real key. We had laundry baskets throughout the house and I could walk by the white laundry bin six days a week and never, not once, think, "the load is getting high." Only on Monday did I switch on the gear that told me to wash, dry, fold and put away the white laundry.

Shopping is simplified on this system. Honestly, we knew what we needed to buy, and kept a piece of paper handy for anyone to fill in the details. By decluttering our minds of all the chores we didn't need to worry about and all the food we didn't need to buy, we had managed our options.

A shopping list that reflects a menu allows you to spend your precious time and mental energy on making steak selections rather than standing in the aisle thinking "What was that? What am I forgetting?" The list frees up mental space.

Years ago, Lindsay said she was sick of eating steak on Mondays. For me, if you recall, all of this is managing options, not managing compromises. So, I said "Fine, what would you like instead?" She said, "Not steak."

You see, I was being channeled into a compromise. I told her anything she came up with would be fine, just let me know exactly what it is. We ate steak on Mondays for a few more years after that. It still doesn't matter what we decide to eat for any meal, let's just make sure we shopped for it, have the items for it, and serve it on time.

Etching is the primary technical tool for managing options. It's reinforced when the coach and athlete can both look at a checklist to insure that everything is being covered. Listen, it comes down to this: Excellence is the race to 10,000 reps a year or 10,000 hours of practice (read the three books that all came out together a few years ago that all said the same thing). I argue that simplicity will get you to that magic 10,000 faster than complexity. I could be wrong, but I think I have proved it with my athletes.

Once you pick an approach, you can then use the checklist—menu, shopping list, playbook, recipe, coaching points—to implement the idea. We want important things in life to be repeatable. I want my throwers to succeed and pass down their insights to the next generation of throwers. I want my family fed by about six every night so we can enjoy a few quiet hours together.

The checklist shows us the path to etching!

Rituals

Rituals are checklists "alive." I am a huge believer in them. As a teacher, I began each class with a short prayer—

Lord, the sea is so large and our boats are so small.

Amen!

Then I would clap my hands and we would go. Students have done amazing imitations of me and they are always based on this little ritual I used to kick off class.

The ritual is, in a sense, the checklist in action, so some of my checklist thoughts and ritual thoughts interconnect. Think about a wedding and the dozens, if not hundreds, of details that must be taken into consideration. Wise ministers will put a little PostIt note in the prayer book reminding them of the names of the bride and groom, as under pressure it's not unusual to forget the names of people you've known all their lives. So, in the middle of a ritual…checklists.

Rituals also inform you it's time to get going. A coach once asked me when I started preparing for a track meet. I thought backwards from the throw and realized that it was when I took Sugar-Free Orange-Flavored Metamucil in the few days leading up to any competition. For me, tasting that tangy orange powder begins the process of preparing me for competition. Much like you start a meal with prayer not only to thank God, but also to let everyone know it is time to eat!

I have so many small rituals—like smiling before I throw— that I think I might overwhelm myself with all of them. Except they work! Why not write everything in a ritual? Because it can be so much information that you get lost in the details and lose the mission or the goal. I smile before I throw, but that's not on my checklist. Sometimes, a ritual is just that—something we do when we do it.

I won a poetry contest years ago with a poem about tossing a handful of dirt on my mother's grave. I just stood there for a moment, then reached over and tossed a handful of dirt. Father Daniel Derry and my cousin, Bill Spillane, both told me, "We didn't know how Irish you were." I had no idea why I did it, it was totally spontaneous and all I can think, still to this day, is it was something I saw others do. That's where rituals live when done best: They sit deep inside you and well up from that place when you need calming and control.

Really, the best rituals are etched so deep, you often don't know how they got there.

Deliberate Practice

To ingrain etching and ritual, I believe in something best described as deliberate practice. I don't like the term so much, but I haven't thought of a better one yet. I first heard this idea from the Soviets. They did experiments with soccer players and discovered some guys were scrimmage heroes. This group mastered every skills test, but often failed in games. Another group wasn't up to par in the tests, but dominated the games.

So, a small change was added, a heart rate monitor. They found there are athletes who can dominate something when the heart rate is 90 or so. And, that's very good, thank you very much. The sport, though, was played at, say, 150 beats. Those extra 60 beats a minute completely changed the skill set.

I was told this same thing years ago by a famous basketball coach that one of the three keys to winning basketball games is making free throws when tired. To master a game skill, it helps to be tired when you practice it!

I used to a drill with my football team to practice third down and 15 yards that my assistant coaches hated. If the offense didn't get the yardage, I sent on the punt team and we kicked. Then we repeated third and 15. We did this over and over. Our young assistants *hated* this, but my point was this: When we punt in a game, we often only have nine or 10 guys on the field. We have to *practice* getting the punt team on in realistic settings.

For the record, we no longer had the issue after this drill.

The Utah high school state championships, as deadly boring a two days one can spend, begins at 8:00am on Friday. As soon as I see the schedule, I start bringing those athletes who are called to compete to school early so they'll get used to throwing, jumping or hurdling at an early hour. At this time of the day, bowel movements, warm-ups, breakfast and literally just waking up are all issues. I am convinced I've snuck in a state champ or two simply by teaching the kids they need about an hour to warm up at 8:00am versus five minutes at 2:00pm.

That's deliberate practice, and it is the key to survival in sports, life…and everything.

Squeeze things down. Make checklists and figure out what truly matters. Embrace rituals and use them to stay focused on what's important. Practice deliberately. Pick something and master it. Ignore what doesn't matter.

Manage your options.

Quick Review

The first four tools—

1. What is your goal? (Where's your Point B!!!)
2. Is this a health or a fitness goal?
3. Will this goal allow you to spiral out, to enlarge your life?
4. What quadrant is your goal in?

Tools one through four are ways to find out where you want to go and what that place looks like. The first four tools help us define Point B. The path to our Point B—The Goal—is once again going to be about an honest assessment of where we are right now (Point A). The first four questions are all about setting the groundwork for the success down the road. Next we will begin the process of getting to the nitty-gritty of the plan. The next six tools are about finding out where Point A is.

Coach Stevo

The athlete in Scene Two is lost, the same as in the first example, but he knows exactly where he wants to be. He even thinks he knows where he is despite all the obvious clues that his assessments are off. The athlete is oblivious to the professional advice he is paying for and the pleads of the person closest to him. This is the classic *Intervention* client Dan faces—he knows Point B, but there's no Point A.

I was going to run a sub-three-hour marathon. The numbers were all lining up for the Las Vegas Marathon in December. As part of my training, I had run a 38-minute 10k and even an 86-minute half-marathon. Fifty-mile weeks were a part of my life and I didn't think twice about waking up for those long, slow morning distance runs.

The afternoon runs were when I struggled. At first, it was shin pain, nothing new, but still very annoying. I adjusted my gait to a mid-foot strike after the 10k. POSE method took the pressure off the front of my calves, but soon it was the back of my calves that were starting to nag, then scream at me.

But I was going to run a sub-three-hour marathon.

"No you aren't."

My doctor was holding a picture of my lower legs that some machine spit out.

"You've got tendinosis."

"Can't I take Motrin for that?"

"I said 'tendinosis.' It means you have little tears accumulating in your Achilles tendons. Every time you run, it gets worse. If you keep running, they are going to rupture."

"How much more can I run?"

"Rupture means I get to go looking for them up in the back of your knees."

"Oh."

My doctor's a runner. She got that it wasn't easy to tell a runner not to run. And that it's harder yet for a runner to hear it. The next morning run was pretty hard.

"Sub-three is going to be harder than I thought."

"Why are you still running?"

My wife is not a runner.

"Because I'm going to run sub-three next month. I'm making all my numbers."

"You can't walk. What makes you think you'll be able to run?"

"I'm running 50 miles a week. I ran an 86-minute half."

"Didn't your doctor tell you not to?"

"She didn't tell me not to." (Yes, she did).

"But you can't walk. And you look like crap. I don't like this."

"What are you talking about? I'm in the best shape of my life."

"You can't walk. And you get sick all the time now."

"Just those two times last month."

"And you never want to fool around. I can't remember the last time we had sex."

My training log didn't have that written in it.

"I don't think you should run anymore."

"But I'm going to run a sub-three-hour marathon."

"Not like this, you're not."

Chapter 11

Fifth Question:
How old are you?

ONE OF THE MOST IMPORTANT tools for discovering where you are in your training is finding out where you are in time and space. This point is so simple, I often forget it when I walk others through the *Intervention* program.

Let's get to the age answer right away.

If you are under 18 and in school, you are in Quadrant One. Learn as much as you can about every sport, game and movement, and immerse yourself in everything you possibly can do. Perhaps you were put on this earth to be the greatest kayaker or fencer the world has ever seen, but you need to try out everything to figure that out. Oh, and learn to ride a bike, swim and tumble at this age if you haven't already. These are skills that stay with you forever and, sadly, are occasionally *musts* in life.

If you are over 18 and in a sport where you earn a living, master your techniques and engage every ounce of energy in maintaining your presence in that sport. Congratulations, you made it—now keep it! I include scholarship athletes in this little window of time.

In a sense, some of the gap we have to address with most people is they're older than they actually realize. My father-in-law and I often joke about "who is the old guy in the mirror?" My brain thinks I'm a teenager, but my body has a different idea. This sounds funny, but unless you are registered at a Division One university or are a member of United States Navy or Coast Guard, training like a college football player or a Navy Special Operator means you're skipping over some obvious steps.

If you are over 18 and not making a living in sport, well, welcome to this simple reality: You are in a lifesaving war against the loss of lean body mass and mobility. You must fight the good fight in keeping these. Life, lard and laziness are all conspiring against you in your noble battle to keep yourself as young as you can be, as long as you can. As the great baseball player, Satchell Paige, said, "How old would you be if you didn't know how old you are?"

This is my favorite part of *Intervention*, by the way.

I get phone calls from middle-aged men who want to be training like Division One college football players without the time, body and support staff. Don't act your age, but train your age. Do everything you can to keep or even increase lean body mass and maintain the right amount of mobility.

So, in case you missed this, it turns out nearly everyone reading this book is in Quadrant Three and is in desperate need for mobility and strength work!

Sixth Question:
What do you lift in the weightroom?

NOW THAT WE KNOW what your goals are and where you are in your life, we need to find out how far along you are in the development of the qualities you need to get to your Point B. And if the "A" in Point A stands for anything, it's assessment. We need to assess everybody and as we all say today—*If you ain't assessing, you're guessing.*

Assessment Number One: Mobility and Strength Movements

My tools of assessment are pretty simple. For basic mobility, stability and flexibility, I am a huge fan of the Functional Movement Screen (FMS), the program Gray Cook and Lee Burton created.

I recently sat in a cold, dark auditorium for four days with Gray and Brett Jones at a CK-FMS workshop, which is the Certified Kettlebell Instructor Functional Movement Screen. Although my skill set with the FMS is, at best, rudimentary, I insist on two of the FMS basics for everyone I work with, the Active Straight Leg Raise (ASLR) and the Shoulder Mobility (SM) screens.

True, you could use all seven of the FMS screens and strive for the mantra of '14 and no asymmetries,' the standard results for a cleared exam. In other words, statistically, someone with this score won't get hurt doing a sport. The problem with any score is this: Imagine a fighter who puts bread on the table by fighting. I am not comfortable saying, "Sorry, you can't work because you have a tight calf muscle."

Okay, that was a gross overstatement, but I think you get the point.

The reason I use the ASLR and SM screens is that I get an instant insight into what Dr. Mark Cheng calls the four knots. The shoulders and hips need to be in an interesting balance between tension, mobility, stability, strength and looseness. Like a knot in your shoelace, too loose and it doesn't hold (bad); too tight and you can't untie it (bad). It has to be 'just so.'

In minutes, I can have a handle on the four knots. As Gray and Brett pounded into me, if there are asymmetries between right and left, that's where we begin our work. We'll be doing hip, shoulder and thoracic mobility work probably every day for the next six months, and having a basic starting point will be helpful.

I am two minutes into the screening process and have a basic sense of how much time we need to spend on mobility work. Some people don't need to spend any time on mobility. For others, it going to be part of the beginning, middle and end of every training session.

For more information on screening and assessing, please read Gray Cook's marvelous book, *Movement*. He's the expert; I collect the crumbs from his plate.

Mike Boyle, the great Boston-based strength coach, recently made a point about mobility that deserves a few minutes of thought.

Mike describes mobility like hanging a door. I did this once, hanging a door, and it took all my math skills, my patience and far too many hours to finally get it done. You see, hanging a door means the spaces are 'just enough.' If the door fits perfectly, it opens and shuts with a mere touch.

Mike notes that joint mobility should be the same: It should be just enough. Your joints should move through without hitches or catches or having to slam anything around. It's not competitive; it's enough.

Put this to memory—

With mobility and strength training, enough is enough.

Formal assessments should be a regular part of a training year. Some of the assessments that don't take any energy from the athlete, like the FMS or some of the various flexibility moves, re-assessing once every six weeks is not a bad idea. With other tests of strength, we might re-test every two months or so. So much of the how and when of assessing depends on the skill of the coach or trainer, but in my experience, the best assessments are done by asking questions and watching movement.

And, that is what this is all about.

It's the next part I take real pride in—the Movements Intervention.

Movements Intervention

This idea is based, of course, on the way some addicts are confronted by loved ones about their addictions. I actually see the same thing, in a sense, with athletes. We become so singularly focused on our strengths that we need to have a bunch of people point out our flaws.

The official title in my notes is *Best lifts...oral exam*. My fun little subtitle is *Waddya Bench?* from the classic *Saturday Night Live* telecast.

In just a few minutes, I can usually discover what the focus of the athlete has been, and also see the glaring omissions.

I'm *not* listening for maxes. I'm listening for this list of movements—

1. Push
2. Pull
3. Hinge
4. Squat
5. Walk/Run/Sprint under load (Loaded Carries)
6. And finally, what I call the Sixth Movement. This is rolling, kneeling, single-leg work and all the rest. To assess, I use one thing—the Turkish Getup.

The initial intervention means finding where the blanks are in the training, and building the program from there.

What do I mean?

Usually, and almost universally, an athlete is accomplished with push. I'm talking about things like 90 pushups in a minute or a double-bodyweight bench press. These are numbers that put an athlete at the top of the heap. With some athletes, this overwhelming push emphasis has also lead to mobility issues I would have just discovered in the shoulder mobility screen.

What would a gap for pushing? I don't know, as I've never seen this in an athlete. But it would be something like the inability to do 10 pushups or something along those lines.

Generally, fighter types in the past few years show up very good at pullups. Maybe we can thank Rocky, or the military, but most fighters seem to know how to do pulling motions. Of course, I've always joked it's because of their chicken legs that they can do rep after rep on the pullup.

I'll admit that hasn't endeared me to them.

The hinge is where I start seeing blank looks.

"You know," I say, "...hinge movements."

"Huh?"

I stand up, put my hands at my hip folds, push my butt back and snap forward.

"Swings. Snatches. Cleans. Deadlifts. Jumps. You know, the most basic and most powerful and most important of human movements?"

Nothing.

It's not unusual to find an elite athlete has ignored the explosive snap movement throughout an entire career. I will say, however, since the boom of the kettlebell, many people are now doing dangerous and insane swing-like variations and proper instruction is the first remedy.

This is going to be one of the areas where I can have great impact on the success of an athlete. The metabolic hit of a correct set of swings is shocking, and much more on the conditioning side of strength and conditioning. If all I do is teach a proper swing and encourage some form of deadlift, I know I will make an impact on this athlete.

When I mention the squat, I usually get, "Um, well, uh," or, "Aren't squats bad for you?"

If you haven't figured it out, my list goes from the most common to the least common movements we see in the gym and, one could argue, from the least important to the most important. I'm pretty convinced all five movements are crucial, and having a "I'm the state's best" here and an "um, well, uh" there is pretty telling.

This is where I can really impact an athlete—and quickly—but also make a person very sore. We really must get in and do squat movements every day. Yes, we're going to be doing goblet squats each and every day as long as we need to address this issue.

The final element on the list is to walk, run or sprint under load. The first response I hear is always, "Well, yes, I jog and I do the treadmill."

That's not the same as dragging a sled, pushing a car or carrying a 75-pound pipe up a hill with a sled dragging behind. After someone asks, "What muscle does this build?" I like to lean over and fill a cup with sweat drops and toss it on him. This is the biggest area where I can have immediate impact in an athlete's conditioning level. When this is missing, I guarantee adding it will be the game-changer.

Loaded carries are not, however, an attempt to get someone tired. Loaded walks and sprints seem to do more to expand athletic qualities than any single thing I've attempted in my career, as either a coach or an athlete. It simply changes our ability to handle more load in all the other areas.

Lastly, I will ask if the person has heard of the Turkish getup. Until recently, this triggered an almost universal, "huh?" If someone has never heard of the getup, I have a pretty good idea what I am going to find on the first attempt. Notice I didn't include any one-arm or one-leg work, nor that core stuff. The Turkish getup will be my assessment tool to determine the coordination of all the other 'Sixth' movements.

Usually, by this point in our relationship I have a handle on how to help. The more advanced the athlete, the easier it is for me to see the ideal program. Simply, and if you have been following along you can see this, I find the omissions in training and make the athlete do them. I often argue that I have made my best progress the last few years because I hired a personal trainer, a guy named Buddy Walker. Listen, I can go to any gym in the world and impress people with my pressing. But the last thing I need to do is press. I need to do asymmetrical work. I need to work on my upper back. I need to work on opening my joints. Buddy makes me do the things I need to do rather than the things I want to do.

That's the definition of quality coaching and the secret to *Intervention.*

Seventh Question:
What are your gaps?

Assessment Number Two: Mobility and Strength Standards

After determining what movements you are and aren't doing, I need to find out your level of competence at those movements. Over time, I've determined some basic strength standards I trust to tell me something. Mike Boyle has his, as does any good strength coach. It's how we find Point A, and maybe a little about where Point B will be.

Some standards to help you decide where you are—

MEN

    Push

    Expected = Bodyweight bench press

    Game-changer = Bodyweight bench press for 15 reps

    Pull

    Expected = 8–10 pullups

    Game-changer = 15 pullups

    Squat

    Expected = Bodyweight squat

    Game-changer = Bodyweight squat for 15 reps

    Hinge

    Expected = Bodyweight to 150% bodyweight deadlift

    Game-changer = Double-bodyweight deadlift

    Loaded Carry

    Expected = Farmer walk with total bodyweight
    (half per hand)

    Game-changer =Bodyweight per hand

    Getup

    One left and right, done with a half-filled cup of water

The getup standard is odd, but with men the challenge of balancing the half-filled paper cup of water on a fist without cheating by using any fingers through the whole range illuminates issues better. I have a lot of small getup drills that work with most of the failures we find in our little getup test.

What do I mean by 'expected' in the standards above? It's this shoulder-shrugging nod of, "Yes, of course, I can do that."

An untrained man can often do these standards on the first training session, and someone detrained (he took a few years off to build up some belly fat) might be able to do most of these anyway.

If you can do all six movements at a game-changer level, your concerns are not in the weightroom. If you're dealing with a body fat problem, it's diet. If you're failing in sport, it's technical or tactical, but it isn't a weightroom issue. You are clearly strong enough and balanced enough to do practically anything.

When we have a team of people at the game-changer level and find challenges, well, I think we can blame something besides the strength coach for the failure. These are general standards, of course, but the idea is, if you max out one test and fail miserably on the others, it indicates your weakness and your best direction.

Oh, and how far on the farmer walks?

It depends, of course, but at least 20 meters and perhaps 40, although it would be fine to go farther. Few movements provide more bang for the buck than farmer walks, so no matter how you score, keep challenging yourself to go farther.

WOMEN

Push

Game-changer = Bodyweight bench press

Pull

Game-changer = Three pullups

Hinge

Game-changer = 275-pound deadlift

Squat

Game-changer = 135 for five in the back squat

Loaded Carries

Game-changer = 85 pounds per hand

For whatever reason, once women at any bodyweight succeed with these standards, amazing things happen. I regularly ask women and trusted coaches standards about women's and am hoping to have more clarity in the future.

It might simply be this—from my observations, when a female athlete deadlifts over 275 pounds, remarkable things happen in the field of play. It has been my thought that even though women have been lifting for a while, we still don't have enough reliable data or information to have clarity about standards for women.

I remember seeing East German studies on throwers, and the numbers were just all over the place. Certainly getting stronger is a good thing, but reliable raw numbers are hard to come by. I'm hopeful we'll have a more complete set in the future.

At this point your answers might be as far apart as "I have never even heard of this thing" to I am at "game-changer level here." Later, we'll discuss how we grade your work, but, if you simply just can't wait, remember this: What you are *not* doing is what you need to do.

The movements you are ignoring
are the things you need to do!

After we look at the movements in detail, we'll review these numbers and some other examples that may be helpful.

Chapter

Eighth Question:
Are you willing to go back to basics?

CERTAINLY, IF YOU'VE *never* done a movement or you ignore it entirely, you need to do that move. But how do know you're on the right path? How do you know that Point A is getting closer to Point B? Certainly, it is assess, reassess and readdress, but sometimes we need to go back to the basic basics.

I think greatness is usually seen in the courage to master the fundamentals. The great musicians practice scales, while the novice is trying too hard to jam together the next great tune. Mastery of the basics of life is something I explain in every workshop, gathering and class.

For my athletes in the Intervention process, this simple question, "Are you willing go back to basics?" is the key. It practically stands alone. Much of the 10-question toolbox demands that we look honestly about where we are and where we want to go, but this question asks the toughest of all—

Are you willing to go back to the beginning again?
Are you willing to start over, start from
scratch, or Finnegan, Begin Again?

As a strength coach, I think the pillars of proper training are both adherence to mastering the basics and the courage to go back to the beginning whenever necessary to insure perfect movement.

My vision of strength training involves competence in all the fundamental human movements. Due to age, illness or injury, an athlete may have to swim many times in the shallow end of pool with all the new kids, but this is where prolonged careers and repeat champions are born.

In this next section, we will look at ongoing assessment for each movement and how you can progress them.

PART

The Fundamental Human Movements

Push
Pull
Hinge
Squat
Loaded Carry

Push

I do a lot of consultations on the telephone. It's still the best way I know to get a sense of what someone is doing and maybe more importantly, what they think they're doing. Writing email, letters and articles has led me to this inescapable conclusion: Most trainees understand only about 10 percent of what they read. This might explain why a friend of mine did benches and curls on his leg day.

When I first talk to a client, I ask about training background. With rare exception, the following is the first statement—

"My best bench is (insert amount)."

After hearing literally dozens of people sum up their training with a bench press number, I realized that of all the basic human movements—push, pull, hinge, squat and loaded carry—the last thing I should worry about is the push.

But then my clientele got more "special."

A while back, I began working with a guy we'll call Bob, who is 6' 8" and weighs 310 pounds. He is only this light in the off-season, and will bulk up nicely for his job as an NFL lineman. He makes a fair amount of money stopping people from hitting quarterbacks, and he's done the job well enough to wear three Super Bowl rings. He has a few issues, of course…like, he can't straighten his left arm and his right shoulder is a mess.

He's not the only one. I've been working with elite athletes the past few years who simply can't push as well as a normal person. Because of these people, who make a fairly good living using their bodies, I developed a nice little system for bringing the push back into the game.

In a wonderful DVD and manual they call *Dynami*, Gray Cook and Brett Jones offered a teaching progression I've adapted (aka stolen with permission) into this format—

Patterning
Grinding
Symmetry
Ballistic or explosive

I often don't get to the ballistics level with clients, because injuries and other issues from the past tend to keep us from this level. As Gray Cook once told me, "Don't add speed to dysfunction." It's good advice for life, too.

	Pattern	Grinding	Symmetry
PUSH	Planks	Pushups	One-Arm Bench Press
		Presses	One-Arm Military Press

We always start with patterning. In the world of pushes, a plank is the base. Oh, and I also know this: Nobody I know thinks they need to plank. I have a little test I stole from Stu McGill, the great back expert from Canada: If you can't hold a plank for two minutes, either you're obese or your abdominal training is wrong.

Not flawed, mind you...*wrong!*

I use the pushup-position plank (PUPP) for most of my work. A beat-up athlete can almost always still PUPP, and it's fairly easy to blend that with other movements. It's a great rest exercise that makes an easy workout harder. I like to mix swings and goblet squats with PUPPs.

Here's the key: It's getting up and down off the ground that will drive the heart rate through the roof, not the actual plank.

I use every plank imaginable, and all my athletes quickly work toward wall-assisted handstands, too. Once we accomplish this, we move to the King of Planks, the cartwheel.

Yes, I know...no one does cartwheels. But when I first saw Frank Shamrock's training program and saw his use of cartwheels, I was impressed, so I tried them. It was oddly one of the most difficult conditioning workouts of my life. And my shoulders took a workout that shocked me.

It's a rare person who won't gain from more planks in their training. Use planks as a focused rest period by mixing them with a big move, or add cartwheels into your outdoor conditioning. For the injured athlete, planks can be added early in the recovery.

The issue I always deal with is this: There's a belief that the plank, or any patterning exercise, is beginner stuff and not worthy of an elite.

Hear this: We're all beginners when it comes to the quality of movement.

The grind family of exercises is pretty obvious in the push world: pushups, bench press, military press and literally, the list seems endless. 1 am a big believer in both military presses and a bench press variation for the athletes I train.

For most people, the grinding military presses are about all that will be needed. I wish I could say more, but there are far better people to speak about the press than me. I am a big fan of Jim Wendler's 5-3-1 training, and he advocates both presses each week, so I must be in good company.

It's the next step that most people skip, but anyone who wants to hit or throw at high speeds should consider symmetry press workouts. I was first exposed to the one-arm bench press by the late Lane Cannon. We did them in his basement, and there I discovered that my body is one piece.

When I recommend these, I always remind people to keep the free, non-weighted hand free. Don't grab onto anything, just let the hand stay free. This will demand that your body lock up and become solid.

And the one-arm bench press will be one of the greatest ab workouts of your life.

Wake Forest's Ethan Reeves fills in the next part of the equation with his one-armed pressing standards. He believes hoisting 125 pounds for five reps is the gold standard for his athletes. I lowered this to 70 pounds for five reps for our high school boys and 30 pounds for 10 reps for the girls. Oh, prepare yourself before you jump up and try this challenge. With anything around 100 pounds, the weight will really pull your 'off' side around and down the bench. You have to counter it by aggressively squeezing everything from your feet up to deal with the weight. It's a full body lift with heavy weights.

Remember: *Keep the free arm free!*

Here's the deal. If you can do 125 with the right and only 70 with the left, you have issues. Now, I don't know what they are, but it's better to find these issues using one-arm work than doing what often happens—adding explosiveness to an asymmetrical issue! Deal with this problem in a systematic approach that includes strengthening the weak side, addressing mobility and flexibility issues, and perhaps even doing some aggressive rehab work.

Fifteen years ago, it was rare to see anyone one-arm overhead press. With Pavel's kettlebell influence, the lift has returned with a vengeance. I am a big fan of this lift and many of my personal workouts are anchored by one-arm presses. It's easy to see asymmetries here. I suggest most men strive for a half-bodyweight one-arm overhead press and, logically enough, to be able to do it with both hands.

In high school, we had a Universal Gym. I don't care if you love or hate machines, but even now when I look back at it, a lot of people trained really hard on the Universal and made pretty fair progress.

One thing we did a lot of was one-arm presses on the military press station. We did them in a way that honestly stands the test of time. I stood in front of the machine and my partner stood nearby with the key.

Now that's an image I haven't used in decades, the key. This was the bent selector key that allowed us to use more than 40 pounds. The coaches kept the keys in the office so no one could use them unless a coach was around. Of course, every kid from Francisco Terrace knew that a bent nail worked just as well, so I had my own personal gym any time I could sneak in.

So, I would do five reps with the right arm. My buddy would move the weight to 50 pounds. Five more reps. We continued this process all the way down the stack until I couldn't do five reps. Then the fun started. We'd go back up to stack, 10 pounds at a time, to the starting weight of 40 pounds. We called these burnout sets, and the shoulder pump was unbelievable.

Of course, now you don't need a partner for that—you just put your left hand on the weight stack and changed the weights all the way down and back up. It worked well then, and I imagine the human body hasn't changed that much, so it might well be worth a try today. You certainly can go up and down the dumbbell rack, or do like we do at my training group with a row of kettlebells on the ground doing the same basic workout.

The varsity throwers at my school came up with a nice twist on this to help the shot put. They only did singles, but changed the reps in a wild, chaotic way each and every rep. There's gold in this idea for throwers, which I ignored most of my career—the variation of speed is an excellent supplement for a thrower or fighter. Alas, I forgot to use it, but perhaps the next generation of elite throwers will remember.

One of the things we all noticed from doing these one-armed workouts is how sore we'd get around the waist.

Growing up, we called the area between our ribs and hips the 'waist.' Now, we call it the core and charge a lot of money to help you train it.

And this is part of the point of doing single-arm overhead work: It challenges you from your toes to the top of your head. Now, I'm not calling for us to start dressing like Ye Olde Tyme Strongman with leopard prints and a saucy mustache, but there's a great tradition in strength sports to put weights overhead one-handed. Like every great lifting idea, it has ebbed and flowed through its popularity.

I see five advantages to one-arm pressing.

First

The whole body is supporting the work done by one limb. This allows us to use more weight with one hand than we can handle with two.

Let's make that a little more clear.

If I can one-hand press 110 pounds, I have two legs and one torso supporting it.

If I put 110 pounds in *each hand*, I still have two legs and one torso supporting it. Now, I know I can press 110 with one hand, but double-110s—220 total—would be a great challenge. My deltoids, triceps and the whole gang of muscles supporting this one-arm lift are really tested.

Yes, you actually overload the arm, if you go heavy enough, by doing one-limb movements. True, the total amount is higher with two arms, but the local load is heavier with one. For hypertrophy, it almost feels like cheating.

Second

This should be no surprise, one-arm lifting is asymmetrical. The bottom line is this—*Asymmetrical work is harder.*

I strongly recommend either using a partner or a mirror when one-arm lifting. I look for the Chin, Sternum and Zipper line, my CSZ Line, to basically remain in vertical while pressing. There will be some twisting and turning under great loads, but limit the twists from vertical as best you can.

I was recently asked, "What do I do when I start twisting?"

"Stop."

I thought I was brilliant.

Third

Equipment needs for one-arm lifts are fewer.

At my old gym, I had 113 kettlebells, but a group of them were far too light for pressing. To have 40 athletes all pressing double kettlebells, we had to share and that, of course, was fine. But by using singles, the whole group could lift at once. There's something magical about watching that many people intensely focused on pressing weights up and down.

Fourth

With a light load and using only one limb, there's a sense of active rest.

Pavel has this funny story about the military—

> *A bunch of privates are shoveling dirt. After a few hours, one of them asks, "Sir, when do we rest?"*

The officer answers, "Ah. If you throw the dirt farther,
the dirt will be in the air longer. You can rest when the
dirt is in the air."

My vision of rest during one-arm lifts seems about the same as in that joke. You rest while the other limb is working. The funny thing is, the body seems more than able to support rep after rep by switching hands. Of course, the reps are challenging as you move along, but that brings us to the next and final point.

Fifth

One-arm pressing naturally leads to longer sets. If time under tension or load is the key to bodybuilding or hypertrophy, alternating hands and continuing to move will certainly increase time. Call Einstein for the specifics on increasing time, but those who have ever had a limb in a cast know that working on the healthy arm or leg seems to keep the atrophy of the injured side to a minimum. The body is one magnificent piece with only a single blood system, and hypertrophy could come with these longer sets.

In my experience, and in those willing to try it, we think it works.

I believe in doing one-arm presses standing. I've done them seated, for example after a surgery, but there's a value to doing them with the whole body wedged underneath the kettlebell.

If you've never done these before, keep the reps low, maybe two to five reps, and get used to the movement. I strongly suggest keeping the elbow vertical under the wrist as in the bench press. Again, a mirror can help here.

There are some variations in position that I use in teaching this—with interesting names like the bottom-up press and the waiter press—but most of the time, just strive to keep the elbow in line with the wrist.

For the older trainee, the one-arm press works all the muscles Vladimir Janda taught us will weaken with age. In other words, if a 50-plus man asked me 'that question'—*If you could only do one lift, what would it be?*— I'd answer, "One-arm presses."

Yes, it even works the glute, as you can't have a saggy butt when pressing half-bodyweight overhead with one arm.

Experiment with increasing your one-arm pressing volume. There's no contest or gold medal for one-arm pressing, but the rewards are great.

If you have symmetry, you may move up to the push-press or other explosive moves. However, I strongly suggest holding off on ballistic movements until you have symmetry with the other basic human movements, especially the pull and the hinge.

So, there you go. The press is most people's favorite move, but there's still a need to look at the push from the lens of patterning, grinding and symmetry. There are few things more rewarding than holding a big lift overhead or nailing a big number in the bench press. Long-term improvement can come from including some work with planks and one-arm presses in addition to the countless sets of bench presses.

Your shoulders will thank me, too.

The gap between fitness and fatness seems to widen each day. It seems each year obesity numbers grow in ways that stagger future medical care. With everyone in the diet, food and fat-loss industries tied to the money-bag in this game, rarely do we hear nutritional advice that isn't immediately countered by another expert.

Pull

I recently read that we each eat about one-30th the amount of cabbage we used to eat, and foods like turnips and beets are vanishing from the table. (Please, I am not advocating a cabbage, turnip and beet diet, although it's better than some of the food plans we see.) Instead, we eat corn sugar and cheap carbohydrates that turn us into the balloon-people look we see at the mall.

Yet in the fitness industry, those who are fit struggle more and more with physical issues that could just easily be addressed but rarely are. In this case, I'm talking about the apostrophe, the sunken chest or the grandpa walk. In other words, the massive number of horizontal pressing movements most people do and an ignorance of horizontal rowing has led us to athletes with shoulders rolled forward, necks craned ahead and shallow chests.

Not only does it look old and morbid, it really impacts athletic success.

The amazing thing is there isn't anything easier to fix. Now, I hear the argument all the time, "Hey, I do rows!" Sadly, most people row in a way that's so dynamic, Olympic lifts seems slow in comparison. The biceps and lower back get dangerously close to injured and the key pulling muscle continues to nap.

I know almost zero about anatomy (although I know what I like; I will wait as you chuckle yourself to a stomach cramp), but there's a funny little muscle in your back called the rhomboid. The rhomboid is like the designated driver: You really should appreciate it, but, well, you forgot.

The rhomboid is there to retract the shoulder blades, but it seems glad to let momentum do the work. It was classified by Dr. Vladimir Janda, the Czechoslovakian neurologist and exercise physiologist I mentioned a few pages ago, as a fast twitch muscle, what he called a phasic muscle—one that weakens with age or neglect.

And ignoring the rhomboid will age you.

If you want to look instantly younger in 10 days, fall in love with the rhomboid. With a few simple moves, you can re-pattern things, build yourself up, check for side-to-side issues, add years to your training and take years off your posture.

A typical workout ignores the rhomboids. Developing this mid-upper back muscle will balance your workout and help you stand taller. Moreover, most guys struggling to gain lean body mass also seem to have posture issues...that lead to soft-tissue issues...that lead to long-term issues.

Let's fix this now.

	Pattern	Grinding	Symmetry
PULL	Batwings	Rows Pullups— *Ab wheel style, details to follow*	One-Arm Plank Rows

We always begin with the pattern. In the basic pull, we have ingrained ourselves toward using speed and momentum to ignore our weaker little areas—or maybe that's just me. And that leads to some real issues. The basic patterning movement I use for pulls is my new standby, the batwing.

Batwings

Here's how to do these. Grab a heavy pair of kettlebells or dumbbells and lie face down on a bench, resting the weights on the floor below you. Pull the weights up toward your ribcage, squeezing your shoulder blades together for a second at the top. When in doubt, stick your thumbs in your armpits on this drill. From a bird's-eye view, your torso should resemble batwings. It seems to look like batwings from the side. In a way, maybe.

This movement is slight, the weights move up and down only about six inches. The higher you pull, the harder you squeeze your shoulder blades. Perform four or five sets of five repetitions. The reps are simple, something akin to an isometric squeeze.

When I wrote about batwings for the first time, I got an email from a guy asking for a video of how to do them because the picture wasn't good enough. Hey, look, this is an isometric—there's no movement. A video of an isometric would look a lot like a picture. As we say, "I'm just saying."

Certainly, increase the time of the holds and the weights, but err on the side of quality. Anybody can do more bad reps, but quality reps are like sunny days in Seattle—rare, but welcome.

I've recently been experimenting with batwings without weight. It's true it's simple, but the point is easily missed: To begin, lean your back against a wall. Having your feet a foot or two away from the wall is fine, and plank your body. Make sure your glutes are tight. Now press your elbows into the wall until you get into the position of having your thumbs in your armpits. And...hold it.

We discovered that *not* having your head touch the wall helps, as the neck will want to help and we don't want that. That's all the "naked batwing" is, but if you don't feel your rhomboids cramping, you might be missing the idea. To make it harder, adjust your feet. For some people, having a partner push against the elbows is enough resistance to get a feel for things.

An interesting side note: When I train elites in many fields, I often do a bit of voodoo after the first set of batwings, pressing down on the upper middle back. There's a sound like a machine gun and the athlete often states, "Wow, that's what I needed." I'm not recommending popping anyone's back, but this exercise really lights up the amount of tension being held in the upper back.

Honestly, I could just stop here and know I've changed lives. But let's move to the next step. If, and only if, you see some improvements in posture or if—and this happens—people ask if you lost weight "or something," move to the slower, grinding rows. It's not bad for people to say you look better, by the way. It's means your posture and system are moving back into a place.

Horizontal Rows

Many of us need to refocus and redirect our attention on horizontal rows. There are plenty of options now, whereas when I was young we had the Reg Park barbell row and some one-arm variations. There are dozens of machines today that range from simple to complex to Tron-like.

Here's the key, though: Slow down and squeeze at the top. In fact, I like a slight pause, at least a one-count, in the position where you have the bar up at the chest. If you can't do this, either go lighter or end the set.

I discovered an interesting thing lately. The issue with many people's rows is symmetry. I have a fun and simple way of testing this that I call human plank rows.

Pullup

The grinding standard for me in testing the pull has always been the pullup. This isn't a perfect solution—I work with athletes who can do lots of pullups, but also look like they're about to tumble forward because of such awful posture. But, there's a value to pullups. Josh Hillis notes that a woman who can do three pullups and three dips almost always has her bodyfat issues locked down. Strength in this movement seems to have an odd correlation with a woman being "rockstar fit," as Josh says.

If a man can't do a pullup, there are obvious issues. Wil Hefernan notes that if you can do 15 pullups, you're probably able to do anything most sports require. It's this rub, this tension between none and too many, that causes the most confusion in supporting athletes.

What happens is we have these extremes of people who can do either no pullups or can crank through dozens. At least, that's what they tell me.

It's a rare person who can't use more pulling work, and this basic pulling move remains a fine test. Certainly, there are some who overdo it, but, again, that's rare.

I was recently reminded by Pavel of the great value of the ab wheel, but you might miss the point: The ab wheel is the right way to do a pullup. The tension on the whole anterior chain should be so locked down that the whole body becomes part of the movement. Having said that, we can now insert all the jokes about ab wheels.

Middle-aged men should do five ab wheels for every pullup. Why? I am raising money to cure MAPS. This is also known as Middle-Aged Pullup Syndrome. After a certain birthday, doing reps in this move starts to make the elbows bark. I took a hint from Pavel on this and keep my reps at two or three, and do lots of sets. This doesn't hurt my elbows and it keeps me in the game. Don't do high-rep pullups if your elbows ache when you do them. This will not get better with more reps.

By doing the ab wheel work, we're getting the benefit of the pullup without the elbow issues. If you get the elbow bite, it's going to be a while before you can really do pullups again. Err on the side of caution here and do less rather than more.

One-Arm Plank Rows

This one is easier to do than to explain. Grab the hand of a good friend or a sturdy post with one hand. Now, with a perfect plank with absolutely no rolling or sway, lean away from your partner until you have a perfectly straight but packed arm. Now row yourself back to vertical. If one side can't hold the plank or rolls out at any point, well, there you go—you have symmetry issues.

I fix the symmetry issues in the basic way—do more reps on that side. Here's the million-dollar secret: Don't do a set of 20 reps. To fix symmetry issues, do 20 sets of one. It's a mental change that leads to a very quick fix of this problem. Rather than bashing through a set, stop and refocus each and every rep.

And it works.

If you have asymmetries, crashing and bashing through set after set of barbell rows is going to lead to you looking up at me and whining, "This is killing my lower back." Don't do that!

Once you reawaken your rhomboids, pause in your grinds and achieve symmetry, you might find a lot of your nagging nonsurgical injuries will ease. You might actually find it harder to discover as many hot spots to foam roll, and your chiropractor visits may be cut way down. What's amazing is that this approach can work wonders in just a few weeks.

The Hip Hinge

	Pattern	Grind	Asymmetry	Ballistics
HIP HINGE	Hinge Assessment Test	Bulgarian Goat-Bag Swings	One-Arm Hinge (Deadlift)	Swings

I am going to tell you about the single most powerful thing you can do and yet sadly, most people have no concept of how to do it.

It's the hinge.

It's the hip snap, the hip slam and all of the various inappropriate terms coaches have used to teach young virgin ninth graders to tackle like NFL linebackers. Just learning the move right can open up hamstring flexibility. Doing it slowly with a massive load can impress your friends for generations. Learning to have symmetry in the movement can jumpstart you to an injury-free career.

And, to do it fast? It's the one-stop shop to fat loss, power and improved athletic ability. Swings, the top of the food chain in hinge movements, are the most under-appreciated move in life, in sport and in the gym.

The metabolic hit of a quality set of swings is shocking, and is much more on the conditioning side of strength and conditioning. If all I can do is teach a proper swing and encourage some form of deadlift, I know I will be making an impact on an athlete.

Breon Hole was struggling with her kettlebell swing and Josh Vert asked me to help out because her lower back screamed after a few repetitions. Within two reps, I stopped her with, "Swings don't hurt your back; whatever you're doing hurts your back."

Breon asked, "Well, what am I doing wrong?"

What I discovered was this: I could *see* the problem, but I had no ability to fix it. I knew drills and we could have pushed, pulled and prodded her to better movement, but I was struggling to explain the problem to her.

Breon was bending her knees too much, which let the kettlebell go too low, which tossed all the forces toward her lower back. It's sometimes called the squatting swing.

When I said that out loud, my little world of lifting had absolute clarity.

You see—

The swing is not a squat.
The squat is not a swing.

It was the greatest insight of my teaching career. We went to a white board and began talking about this notion. It soon became known as the hip displacement continuum.

The Hip Displacement Continuum

Within a few minutes, I posted a first tickler of the idea at my forum at *davedraper.com.*

Breon and Josh Vert asked a good question, we worked it through, and then I called Mark Twight to talk about this continuum concept. Breon had been taught to do swings from a deep squat and was told, "You're cheating if you don't deep squat."

Well, no...

Put this on a rainbow curve or continuum.

On the far left: Swings

On the far right: Goblet squats

Swings   Goblet Squats

The most powerful movements the human body can achieve are from this swing position or, as it has been called more recently, the hinge movement.

Pavel has added much to this concept. Hinge movements, like the swing, have deep hip movement and minimal knee bend. Squat movements have deep movements in both the hip *and* the knee.

So, to memorize—

Hinge the hips (swings, jumps) means maximal hip movement, minimal knee movement

Squats mean maximal hip movement, maximal knee movement

If you're walking and a rattlesnake crosses your path, that leap away will be more on the hinge side of the continuum. If you first wish to kiss the rattler, that movement would be a squat. You decide, but I have no question about which I would do.

Bad jumpers start with a lot of knee bend and diminish the pop of the hinging hips. Bad squatters bend their knees a lot and ignore the hip movement. The continuum clarified this thinking for me forever. It's one of the few times when mental effort can improve physical performance.

As a test, we added a series of standing long jump tests. First, we encouraged the athlete to use a lot of knee bend and "really use your legs" and tested three jumps. Then, we asked for nearly no knee bend, but a snappy hip movement. Most athletes are within three inches of their best with this style and many athletes actually do better.

Finally, allowing some additional knee bend but emphasizing the explosive hip, the athlete takes a few more attempts. It's more common than not to reach personal records here.

Pavel calls the stiff-legged swing 'the tipping bird,' like those old bar standards where the plastic bird swings back and forth into a drink. As you move across the continuum, you might note that the knee bends more and more, but it's never none. There always needs to be a slight bend in the knees during any movement. One of the great errors of beginning squatters is to lock the knees at the start or top of the movement.

No need to jack up your knees for life: Keep a slight bend.

It's interesting to think about the popularity of leg extension and leg curl machines in the '70s and '80s. These use no hip or deep knee bending, but there has been some research indicating these movements are terrible for the knees. Mother Nature seems to know best when it comes to training.

When people complain that swings hurt the low back, it's often because they have turned the movement into a squatting swing. Always attack the zipper, hinge the hips, make the hips fold...or whatever clue helps you.

When people complain that squats hurt their knees, take a moment to cue the hips. The hinge is achieved by *pushing the butt back*. When first learning, most people will excessively bend the knees. You truly need minimal knee bend.

Here's the formula, again.

Squat: Maximal Knee Bend and Maximal Hip Bend
Hinge: Minimal Knee Bend and Maximal Hip Bend

Patterning the Hip Hinge

The hinge is more powerful than the squat. The hinge is the vertical jump, the standing long jump, the snatch, the clean and the swing. It's the tackle and the check in hockey. Get that image in your head, not a slow squatty move, but rather a dynamic, butt back into hip snap. Get that image.

The patterning is so important that I use the following drill nearly daily.

Stand next to a wall, facing away. Hinge at your hips so your butt touches the wall. Step about six inches from the wall and repeat the butt touch. Move an inch or two more and repeat. Keep doing this—touch the wall and scoot a little out a little more.

When you really feel your hamstrings burning and shaking, you have it right. Like a bow and arrow, those strings can deliver an unbelievable amount of power.

It might sound odd to pattern the hinge, as it's as natural as relieving yourself. But when we add load, many people cheat themselves by not pushing the butt back and instead use the quads as the focus.

For stubborn clients, and usually this is a woman's issue, I use the HAT, the Hinge Assessment Test. It is brutal to explain, but simple to demonstrate and we have a video example on *YouTube*—
http://youtu.be/34saz57cxjs

Whereas a picture is worth a thousand words, this video trumps that too.

Grinding the Hip Hinge

The next movement will both teach and train you. After patterning, let's work on grinding. Grinding in our world means slow strength moves that do wonders for patterning, but also deliver a lot of metabolic work and, obviously, improve strength.

To grind the hip hinges, use a heavy sandbag, a kettlebell or a plate, hug the weight to your chest, keeping the weight basically at your sternum and upper abs. Now, repeat the hip hinge, still holding the weight to your chest. I usually do a set of five of the grinds, then repeat the wall drill.

This movement, which I get a kick out of calling the Bulgarian goat-bag swing, is an excellent way to slow down the hinge movement and teach the keys to more dynamic work. Here we're looking for pressurized breathing, the correct feeling of the hinged hip, and the abdominal tightness that insures stability. For a swift workout nearly guaranteed to steam up your hamstrings, do these hip hinge grinds for reps, 5-10-15-15-10-5.

Alternatively, the deadlift is an excellent grinding option. For years I've insisted upon a double-bodyweight deadlift as the rule of thumb to indicate someone is beyond the beginner stage. It's a good measure of overall body strength, grip strength and appropriate training. Women seem to do well in sport with 150% of bodyweight, but I've noticed, almost without exception, when a woman deadlifts 275 and above, good things happen in sport.

Before we move on to the million-dollar move, let's take a few minutes to check symmetry. You'll need a mirror and a single kettlebell. Hold the kettlebell in one hand and practice the hinge pattern. Again, if you have to re-pattern the hinge with the wall drill and some Bulgarian goat-bag swings, that's fine.

Watch for the CSZ line—the "chin, sternum and zipper" line—which should all remain in a single vertical line. With the kettlebell in hand like you'd hold a suitcase, do several hinges. As most readers know, I am a big fan of single-arm moves, but this one really helps tie down the opposite side. If you see yourself pulling offline, re-pattern the first two drills.

The Swing

Finally, we get to the swing. If I had to pick one move that will burn fat, loosen the hips and legs, and raise the buttocks to an eye-pleasing height, it would be the swing. Remember, if you haven't worked on your patterning, grinding and symmetry, take the time to do it first.

If you do swings correctly, it is your one-stop shop for general training. Done correctly, swings are the ticket to fat loss, as well as sore glutes and hammies. But, "done correctly" is the key here. The swing can be taught horrifically. A TV expert—you know the one—came out with a DVD on kettlebells, and the swing technique in it is literally immoral.

The swing is a simple move to look at from the side, but a little difficult to learn. Securing some competent instruction is worth the time, energy and money.

There is a new study from the American Council on Exercise Research, "We know the kettlebell swing actually is the best fat loss movement there is."

And,

"Kettlebell workouts burn 20.2 calories per minute. That's double Spinning (9.8 calories per minute) and that's double traditional boot camp workouts (9.9 calories per minute)."

Your standard should be being able to do a workout of 75–250 swings and not be sore the next day. The range of 75–250 is a large enough spread so those who swing big kettlebells for strength or light kettlebells for fat loss are all included.

That range is an odd way to have a standard, but as I tell people, if your low back hurts after swings, it's *your* fault. Soreness in the lower back after swinging often indicates poor hinge mechanics. And we can't have that.

I think you can get away with as little as 75 swings, three days a week. I made a goal of 250 swings a day one month and everybody asked me about my diet. It was awful and I ate and drank too much, but I started looking pretty good from that little project of 250s.

Swings work that well.

One route is to come up with a number, 75 is excellent for beginners, and break it into bite-size sets or 20 or 25 swings.

My favorite workout is "I go/You go" with this rep scheme—
5-10-15-15-10-5

That's 60 reps and the rest period is only a few seconds. If it's true that we need to teach our hearts to climb and then recover quickly, well, here's my contribution. Although you can do this up to five rounds, try it first, and then make plans for dinner and dancing. Maybe.

30/30 also works well. Thirty seconds of swings, followed by 30 seconds of rest is a marvelous way to get a lot of work into a short period of time. If all you have is 10 minutes, try the 30/30. Toss in a set of farmer walks and you've taken care of business.

The hip hinge is as good as it gets for the human body in terms of performance. Take the time to walk through the basics, as I do nearly every workout for both myself and the good people I work with here and there.

The challenge is simple: *Do this!*

The Squat

	Pattern	Grind	Symmetry
SQUAT	Doorknob Drill Goblet Squat	Double KB Front Squats Front Squats Back Squats Overhead Squats	Single-Side Squats

The greatest impact I've had on strength and conditioning starts with a story.

Years ago, faced with 400 athletes who couldn't squat correctly, I attempted to teach the squat, move after move, lift after lift.

I failed each and every time.

I saw glimmers of hope from teaching one kid the Zercher squat (weight held in the crooks of the elbows...enjoy!), and a few picked up the pattern when we lifted kettlebells off the ground by the ball, called potato sack squats since they look like picking up a sack of potatoes off the ground. But nothing was working.

Somewhere between a Zercher and a potato squat was the answer.

It came to me when I was resting between swings with the weight held in front of me like I was holding the Holy Grail. I squatted down from there, pushed my knees out with my elbows and, behold, the goblet squat!

Yes, the squat is that easy. It's a basic human movement and you just have to be reminded how to do it.

Squats can do more for total mass and body strength than probably all the other lifts combined. Doing them wrong can do more damage than probably all the other moves, too.

Let's start simple. Find a place where no one is watching and squat down. At the bottom, the deepest you can go, push your knees out with your elbows. Relax…and go a bit deeper. Your feet should be flat on the floor. For the bulk of the population, this small movement—driving your knees out with your elbows—will simplify squatting forever.

Next, try this little drill. Stand arms-length from a door knob. Grab the handle with both hands and get your chest up. Up? Imagine being on a California beach when a swimsuit model walks by. When I have an athlete do this, immediately he puffs up his chest, which tightens the lower back and locks the whole upper body. The lats naturally spread a bit and the shoulders come back a little.

Now, lower yourself down.

What people discover at this instant is a basic physiological fact. The legs are not stuck like stilts under the torso. Rather, the torso is slung between the legs. As you go down, leaning back with straight arms, you'll discover one of the true keys of lifting—

You squat between your legs.

You do not fold and unfold like an accordion—you sink between your legs.

Don't just sit and read this: *Do it!*

The Goblet Squat

Now you're ready to learn the single best lifting movement of all time—the goblet squat. Grab a dumbbell or kettlebell and hold it against your chest. With a kettlebell, hold at the horns or with a dumbbell, just hold it at one end, vertical, like you're holding a goblet against your chest.

You see—goblet squats.

With the weight cradled against your chest, squat down with the goal of having your elbows slide past the inside of your knees. Your elbows are pointed down, and it's okay to have them push against your knees, pushing your knees out as you descend.

There is the big-money key to learning movements in the gym—let *the body* teach the body what to do. Listen to this: *Try to stay out of it!* Thinking through a movement often leads to problems; let the elbows glide down by touching the inner knees and good things will happen.

The more an athlete thinks, the more we can find ways to screw things up. Don't believe me? Join a basketball team and get into a crucial situation. Shoot a one-and-one with three seconds to go, down by two points, and get back to me later if you decided thinking was a good idea.

I'm not sure I should tell you this, but here it is: I think goblet squats are all the squatting most people need. If the bar hurts in back squats (I won't comment), your wrists hurt in front squats (swallowing my tongue here) and the aerobics instructor has banned you from using the step boxes for your one-leg squat variations, try the goblet squat. Seriously, once you grab a kettlebell over 100 pounds and do a few sets of 10 in the goblet squat, you might wonder how the toilet got so low the next morning.

As a simple guide for foot placement, do three consecutive vertical jumps, then look down. This is roughly where to place your feet every time you squat. You know the toes should be out a little, and most people look down and see the toes magically out. You don't want to go east and west here, but you want some toe-out.

There is an important coaching point to be made. The goblet squat and all the drills I've described teach patterning. Unless you have the pattern, you shouldn't move into heavier work. I am to the point where I even hold off front and back squats until a person can prove the stability, flexibility and, most importantly, the patterning of the squat.

Double-Kettlebell Front Squats

After the goblet squat, we're now moving to the grind squats movements—the slow strength moves—like the double-kettlebell front squat (DKFS). The load remains in front, which insists that the whole core be rigid. Moreover, with two kettlebells, you can still have your elbows down to push the knees out.

DKFS are exhausting in an odd way: Like wrestling an anaconda, you seem to be slowly choking yourself to death. The pressure is also teaching you to stay tight as you continue to grease up and down. Also, the DKFS seems to really work the upper back in the style of compression. This is a forgotten method of muscle and strength building where the constant squeezing of a muscle system is the movement, for lack of a better term.

As a grinding standard, we can certainly expect a bodyweight squat within a short amount of time after the pattern is established and the athlete moves into grinds. Again, as I noted in the standards, if you can do 15 reps with your bodyweight on your back, you're probably strong enough to do just about any sport.

Single-Side Squats

Single-side squats provide a unique way of strengthening the whole body with weight just on one side. It is a simple movement: Grab a single kettlebell and clean it. With the kettlebell tight to the body—I recommend the thumb touching the upper pec and the forearm tight against the body—squat down.

Remember the CSZ idea from the hip hinge? We use the same tool here. With the load just on one side, there is some twisting and pivoting by the body. The Chin-Sternum-Zipper line should be vertical all the way up and down.

If not, why isn't it?

When I really injured my leg years ago, I thought rehabbed it perfectly. Yet I couldn't get my body *not* to twist away (left hip injury, my body turned to the right in the bottom position of the single-side squat). It took an expensive medical intervention to deal with the problem, and today I have a perfect CSZ at the bottom of my single-side squat. Thankfully, early on I didn't add ballistics to this dysfunction because parts of my body might have come off!

Loaded Carries

There's something I've discovered that does more to expand athletic qualities than any other thing I've attempted in my career. There is no question that tapping into the right movement can radically change an athlete. Famously, I went from a bodyweight of 162 pounds to 202 in four months when Dick Notmeyer graciously insisted that I squat deep and often. Even though I was stronger in the bench press than most mortals, my lack of squatting kept my bodyweight in a range more appropriate for a skier than a discus thrower.

A few years ago, I worked with a guy named Ted (not really, but you get the idea). Ted's issue was interesting: He was a fairly solid powerlifter (bench press, squat and deadlift), and very good at the two Olympic lifts—the snatch and the clean & jerk. In other words, he was not a wannabe, a beginner, a neophyte, nor a internet warrior. Ted is the real deal.

When he came to visit with me for advice, there wasn't a ton I could help with in the weightroom. A point here and an idea there, and I was pretty much finished. So, being finished, we went outside to do what some people used to call a finisher.

"Would you rather do carries, walks or sleds?" I asked.

"I've never done any of that kind of thing."

Good, I thought. I can help.

Within seconds of his first attempt with the farmer bars weighing 105 pounds each, he was a stumbling drunk. Of course, in a few hours after several drinks and lots of discussion, we both would be that way.

He could pull hundreds of pounds off the floor, but didn't have the stability—the cross-strength—to handle more than a few feet with the bars. We tried a heavy carry, and he was gasping for breath like being choked by having to squeeze the 150-pound bag to move. Literally, his human inner tube had almost no range past five seconds.

Yeah, I can help.

A few weeks later, I answer the phone to a call I have heard before, "Dan, you're a genius (humbled coach blushes, but nods knowingly). My deadlift has gone up (low 500s to high 500s) and I am just thicker all over."

I'm not surprised. Again, in my career of coaching and lifting, *nothing* in my toolbox has been a game-changer like loaded carries.

Loaded Carries

I break the carries into three categories. Actually, it's four, but you'll see the point.

Weights in Hand

These are the simplest and most recognized—grab one or two dumbbells or kettlebells and walk away.

One-Handed Carries

Waiter Walk—The weight is held with an arm straight overhead like a European waiter in a café. This is usually the lightest of the carries and does wonders for shoulders.

Suitcase Walk—This is like moving through the airport, grab the weight in one hand like a suitcase and walk. The obliques on the other side of the weight will want to have a discussion with you the next day.

Rack Walk—These are usually done with a kettlebell, holding the kettlebell in the racked position, which is the weight on your chest as if in a 'clean' position. This is a fairly remedial move, but it can teach a person how the abs work.

Two-Handed Carries

The Press Walk—This is a double-kettlebell waiter walk, but the kettlebells come alive as you move. Do not do this to failure—it looks dangerous because, well, it is.

Farmer Walk—The King of Carries. Go as heavy as you can with kettlebells in both hands like a double-suitcase carry. This can be done really heavy or for great distance. My favorite variation is really heavy for a great distance.

Double-Rack Walk—Again, this is a learning exercise, but it's a great way to learn to breathe under stress.

Cross Walk—Here we do a waiter walk in one hand while doing the farmer walk in the other. It's a very interesting way to learn to lock down the midsection during movement.

Bags

This group of carries includes backpacks, sandbags or weighted vests. Personally, I still prefer an old duffle bag or field pack. Go to any grocery store and buy either water softener salt or salt for de-icing. For under $10, you can get 150 pounds of salt. Sand works better in many situations, but I always used the de-icer on the driveway during the winter, which served the dual purpose of training and safety.

The basic bag carries are simple. Really, it comes down to either backpacking or holding the weight over the shoulders or bear-hugging the weight. The backpack or vest set-up is ideal, as it leaves your hands free.

Bear-hugging a weight is a great training tool. The internal pressure builds, the breath is choked off by the weight on the chest, and you have to keep squeezing it harder just to keep it off the floor. All in all, it's just nothing but fun.

Sleds

The method is simple: Hook up a sled either with a harness or weight belt and tow it away. Along with sleds, this concept also includes pushing cars, going up hills (forward and backward), and all the various new pushing devices available in today's better gyms.

Each of these work well alone. Combining them makes them worthy of note. Farmer walks with 105 pounds in each hand, with a 150-pound backpack and dragging a sled is one of the most difficult things I've ever done. Obviously, some combinations don't work as well as others—crosswalks and overhead walks of any kind are usually epic failures when combined with something else.

Here's the answer to the question you didn't know to ask—

What's the order of learning all this?

What's the Order of Learning?

LET'S REVIEW the order of learning—

Patterning
Grinding
Symmetry
Dynamic

	Pattern	Grind	Symmetry	Dynamic
LOADED CARRY	Farmer Walks Bag Carries	Car Pushes Prowlers	Waiter Walk Suitcase Walk Rack Walk— *One arm only*	Hill Sprints Sleds— *If technique is correct*

Driving someone too quickly through this progression is fraught with issues. I begin with the farmer walk because it quickly teaches patterning.

I used to correct students for looking over their shoulders and talking to each other, but I realized the bars teach that at a far deeper level. The hair on the top of your head should reach to zenith and your eyes should look just over the cheekbones.

Ideally, I find walking the line, like Johnny Cash did, has a real value in teaching a person posture with a quiet upper body. Honestly, a long and happy career can be had from just doing this walk.

I find walking the line to be a wonderful and easy way to show imbalances. Now, what causes them is certainly an issue, but I find there's a moment of insight ("Oh, I see!") provided quickly by a person struggling to stay on-line. Again, there may never need to be an issue about moving on from here, as these asymmetrical moves will do wonders for the bulk of the population.

Bear-hug walks with heavy bags can be done at the basic level, too. It's a step more advanced than the farmer walk, but this kind of carry really seems to teach pressurized breathing better than any single thing I know.

Once the farmer walk is established, we load up a push. Pushing a car is not a bad start, although today we have plenty of gym toys that don't require a driver and a safe place to push.

Then, for our symmetry work, the waiter walk and suitcase carry quickly expose technical or anatomical issues.

These movements at high speeds, like sprinting with sleds or sprinting up hills, can be incredible for any athlete. I discovered as a high school track coach, we were getting better throwing by having two weekly focused hill-sprint workouts. The volume was low, often only two sprints, but the carryover was obvious. You can think of these as explosive one-legged squats if the hill is steep enough.

I often tell people, if all you can do is farmer walks and hill sprints, you're doing pretty well.

Many people can farmer walk bodyweight, half-bodyweight in each hand, during their first carry workout. There are no perfect standards for loaded carries, as the variations and options seem about endless, but certainly a double bodyweight carry— bodyweight in each hand—is worthy indicator of high levels of strength.

Now, the next issue—

How much and how often?

I've had high school sophomores use 85 pounds per hand in the farmer walk, and my backyard group has worked with up to 155 pounds per hand. I've done more in competition with the farmer bars and wouldn't suggest you do it. Whatever you have at hand is a good start.

A bag of salt or sand weighing 50 pounds is an amazing eye-opener in carries. Go to a warehouse home supply place and get a wheelbarrow shell (just that green part that holds stuff), string a rope through the hole in the wheelbarrow and connect the rope to a weight belt and you have your first sled.

For sled weights, I started out with cement that had been thrown out, and a bunch of rocks.

So, with two dumbbells or kettlebells, a wheelbarrow shell, a weight belt, a backpack, some sand and some rocks, you can train at the top end of the food chain.

How far? How many? How long?

Well, it depends. I usually tell people to first try the farmer walk. Then, pull a bag to your chest and walk around. Don't go far and don't do much, just get a sense of things.

Rarely do we do more than 'down and back' with each move, as we strive to keep adding elements each set. A person who has mastered patterning, grinding, symmetry and ballistics could have a great workout with just 'down and backs' of—

> **Suitcase Walk**
> **Farmer Walk**
> **Suitcase Walk Wearing a Weighted Back Pack**
> **Farmer Walk Wearing a Weighted Back Pack**
> **Sled Pull**
> **Sled Pull with Bag (Bear Hug)**
> **Sled Pull Wearing a Weighted Back Pack**
> **Sled Pull with Back Pack** *and* **Farmer Walk**

That's eight movements 'down and back,' with minimal equipment and a lot of work.

The *how far* question is usually answered "not very." You'll find out why.

Do some kind of loaded carry three times a week, but only one of the days should be 'everything.' You want to be aggressive and intense when you attack these movements. The farmer walk and bear-hug carries are my personal favorite moves and for most people tend to be some of the best bang for their bucks.

Get back to me after doing these for three weeks. Obviously, your grip is better. Your legs are stronger. You discover the weightroom isn't that tough any more. You look leaner but bigger.

Oh, and you're welcome.

Chapter 17

The Sixth Movement

THERE IS AN EXCELLENT QUESTION that comes up in my *Intervention* workshops.

"Dan, what about all the other stuff?"

Oh, I understand this question. You don't see one-arm movements until symmetry, you don't really see one-legged work and what about fill-in-the-blank?

Everything else is the sixth movement. Or, probably more accurately, everything else is the five movements plus one. Half-kneeling presses, landmines, one-armed dive-bomber pushups, chops, rows, cross-plane single-leg deadlift with a row (I call these HATwings), or any time you throw a medicine ball, you're doing the 'sixth movement' or the 'plus one.'

Don't make this a judgment statement. I'm not saying the sixth movement is somehow less than the first five; I'm saying all that other stuff is valuable and needs to trained, but not at the expense of training the hinge or loaded carry.

And we know that the adult population needs a lot of things that are often left out of modern training. There are attempts to address this—you can see people at local gyms lunging a bit here and there, and we see basic correctives done in many facilities.

But rarely do we see people on the floor. I don't think I have ever seen rolling in a public facility, and few people actually get on their backs and do anything save crunches or situps.

If I understand the numbers correctly, 28,000 Americans die each year in fall-related injuries. If you wear your seatbelt and don't smoke, falling is the demon lurking around the corner waiting to take you down. Besides a few railings and a skid-proof mat, what do most people do to prevent or deal with falling?

Nothing.

I use the Turkish getup and drills as my 'plus one.' The getup begins on the floor, often loaded with a kettlebell, and through it we roll, hinge, kneel, lunge, stand and then come back down under control.

Tim Anderson

I asked Tim Anderson, the author of *Pressing Reset,* for some insights about getting us back to basics. Tim believes we need to take things back to when we first popped our eyes open!

Here's Tim—

ONE THING THAT SEEMS to be missing from the majority of the training programs is ground work. Most people don't spend enough time on the ground, or enough time learning to get up off the ground.

Let's look at children, for instance. They build amazingly strong bodies by learning how to maneuver and get up off the ground. They roll, creep, crawl, squat, kneel and eventually learn to stand. In doing so, children develop mobility, stability and strength where they need it.

Most adults do the opposite. We spend most of our time trying to stay off the ground. To be honest, we spend most of our time trying to find conveniences so we don't have to move around very much. In turn, we lose mobility, stability and strength where we need it. We are doing this all backwards.

Perhaps all childish ways were not meant to be put away. If we spent more time on the ground, we could really build a strong and healthy body. This is the reason the Turkish getup is such a great exercise. It gets you back on the ground and allows you to move through several child-like movement patterns. In doing so, you can actually start regaining the mobility, stability and strength you're supposed to have.

Let's take a look at the getup through a child's eyes. It starts from a lying position and involves a roll to a seated position. We then lift from a sitting position to a three-point stance—all but one limb is in contact with the ground, so it is just shy of being on your hands and knees. From the three-point stance, there's a transition to the half-kneeling position, and from the half-kneeling position, we stand.

Basically, the get-up mimics the way a child might go from lying to standing. Holding a kettlebell overhead could even offer similar resistance as a child's heavy, out-of-proportion head. The getup is a great way to intentionally do what children learn to do so well: move from the ground up.

Did I mention children develop amazingly strong bodies?

We adults need to spend more time on the ground. In fact, just getting down on the floor and performing a few resets can go a long way toward building a strong, healthy body. One move I love in particular is done by getting down on hands and knees and rocking back and forth with a tall sternum, meaning a big chest, which I call rocking. Tricky name, I know.

Rocking is a great way to reset your body and clean up your movements. It stimulates the vestibular system—your balance system; it opens up your hips. It's a great way to quickly improve a squat or a swing; it stimulates the muscles in your arms and core reflexively; and it connects your hips to your shoulders. Throw in a couple of neck nods, simply raising your head up and down while on all fours, and you'll light up your core muscles like a Christmas tree!

In other words, rocking helps tie your core together. It truly prepares your body to move.

Another reset I like is rolling. Rolling helps to tie the body together by building rotational strength and stability, thus preparing and enabling the body to transfer force effectively from one side to the other. Simply rolling around on the floor can enable you to become strong. Rolling also stimulates the vestibular system and offers a huge proprioceptive flood of information to the brain—it improves your movement map. The better you roll, the better you will move.

Rolling and rocking are great resets. They can actually help you regain your movement foundation, and make an essential addition to any training program. They really are resets.

And they make a great complement to Turkish getups, which combines aspects of both rocking and rolling.

The bottom line is, any training time spent on the ground is time well spent. Babies and children build strength the right way, and we'd benefit by emulating them. If you want to get stronger or you just want to be healthy, learn how to get up, get down and roll around, to tumble, creep and crawl. Approach movement like a child—like you once did when you could do almost anything.

~Tim Anderson, co-author of *Becoming Bulletproof,* author of *Pressing Reset* and *Fitness Habits Made Easy*

Tim was my partner at a workshop and he honestly gets it. Note the lack of macho posturing in his suggestions and his holistic approach to training any population. To be honest, we sometimes get stuck on weightlifting becoming a war between human and barbell, but most of us also need time to rework and readdress the issues brought on by accidents, injuries and idiocy.

My hand went up first, by the way, when it came to wondering who's had accidents, injuries and idiocy impact their bodies.

The Turkish Getup

Both Tim and I referenced the Turkish getup as a fundamentally simple way to get all of this into your workout. I recommend responsible coaching to help you learn this correctly. It has taken me years to learn the getup, and it took some extra work to learn to teach it correctly.

Honestly, not everyone needs to master the steps of the getup. Let me walk you through my approach with adults.

I begin my teaching of the movement in the six-point position. This is where you're on your hands and knees on the ground—two hands, two knees, two feet; you get it…six points.

Begin by making big nodding movements, shifting the neck up and down, then try to look backward over your shoulders, one side then the other. Then, do what Tim calls rocking, and push your hips back into a gentle squatting motion of the lower body.

It's funny, as most people tell me they can't squat but I can get them rocking on the first attempt.

For many of my adult clients, this will be the most time they've spent on the ground training since forever.

Next, lie on your back. I have one simple rule about the drills on you back: Always rest your head after each rep.

Why?

All too often, adult trainees will use their heads as a jump-start to get the body off the ground. You can see it in the way most people do situps: It looks like a series of crash-test dummies hitting the wall over and over. I don't like the word core, but worse yet, many people have taught themselves that the core is the front of the neck and the lower back. Our job is to literally re-knit the system here.

In Steve Ilg's wonderful book, *Total Body Transformation*, he notes that the word "fit" comes from the old Norse term "to knit." I can think of no better way to explain not only the integrated role of fitness in one's life and community, but also how to think of the core. From your shoulders to your hips, Doc Cheng's four knots, should be like a chain-link fence.

I once came upon a car crash. The car wiped out the supporting posts, but was still held in the flexible but strong knitting of a chain-link fence. This is how your core should react, strong and flexible.

From supine lying, we move to simple rolling. With the elbows at 45 degrees—straight out from the body is 90, straight down along the sides would be zero—slowly climb up on your elbows in a gentle roll.

Remember, head down on each rep! This should be like lying on the floor, then hearing exciting news on the TV: roll up until your elbow is the only part of your upper body still on the ground. Then, roll back down. I call these Rolling 45s.

From here, roll onto your stomach. Here's another trick from Tim Anderson: As you strive to roll over and back by driving the sole of one foot, let's say the right, straight up and let it lead you over to your left. Let the leg be the engine of the role. Just using your legs, roll back and forth, stomach to back, right to left, until you begin to feel your whole body engage.

Don't use your upper body to help!

What we are doing with the early sequence is teaching and reminding the body how to move on the ground. The six-point moves, the rolling 45s and the tummy rolls are great ways to awaken those early primal patterns we all learned as babies.

In the Turkish getup, we discover usually issues. We do literally dozens of partial movements in our gatherings at the Crosspointe Kettlebell Club or the Coyote Point Kettlebell Club.

As Brett Jones reminds us, "This is a drill, not the skill." In my vision, adults need to do many more drills than we often do. So we break down the getup in many ways that often never seem to actually lead anywhere.

Well, it doesn't lead anywhere until the participant moves flawlessly, nearly mindlessly, through the whole movement.

And this is when things get exciting. The sixth move—the five plus one—can be expanded to go far beyond just rolling on the floor.

Coach Stevo

Coach Stevo offers us this—

You know that old expression, "I trust that person about as far as I can throw him"? I think Dan John would trust that person a lot because he can throw heavy things very, very far. But I have a confession to make. I can probably front squat, power clean, bench and carry that person, but I can't throw much of anything to save my life. This is a problem, because like the squat, hinge, push, pull and carry, throwing—the ballistic application of rotational force—is a sixth human movement.

Throwing is ballistic rotation. Everything that leaves your hand leaves on a ballistic trajectory. Force starts at the ground, transmits through the body, and is directed into whatever you want to get rid of through the rotational force of your coordinated muscles around your center of mass. And that includes throwing a punch. Hooks, uppercuts, even jabs involve rotation.

But rotational force is hidden in a lot of other athletic movement. You generate and resist rotational forces when you—

> *Run*
>
> *Jump*
>
> *Change direction*
>
> *Swing anything*
>
> *Serve*
>
> *Volley*
>
> *Kick*
>
> *Tackle*
>
> *Slam*

Dodge

Turn

Pound someone's face

Have sex

Or do anything with one hand or on one leg

As you can see, pretty much every athletic movement involves the application or resistance of rotational forces. So how does one, especially someone like me who never played ball sports as a kid, train this human movement?

For throwing, the progression is as follows—

Roll

Everything starts on the ground. The movement pattern for applying rotational force begins as basic rolling. That's right, we learn to throw by rolling around on the ground as a newborn. The ground provides more stability and allows kids to break down the movement into little parts that we can learn. We roll around using our arms, roll around using our legs, all without the risk of falling over and getting hurt.

The ground also allows us to work against gravity instead of across it, which is a lot more complicated. As adults there are lots of great ways to mimic this progression that also safely increase stability and range of motion along the spine. Here are a few examples from the Coyote Point Kettlebell Club—

> *Lie on your back and roll onto your stomach using only your legs*
>
> *Lie on your back and roll onto your stomach using only your arms*

> *Getup Planks*
>
> *Loaded Cuddles*
>
> *Rolling 45s*
>
> *Rolling 45s to the T*
>
> *Half-Getups*
>
> *Turkish Getups—the ultimate rolling exercise*

Twist

Once we're on our feet, we start twisting in space. To adults, this looks a lot like just moving around, and we barely think about it. We pick up stuff slightly to one side or the other. We put on backpacks. We move gear from one side of a room to another. These are grinding applications of rotational force.

We also resist rotational forces when we work to remain upright in a car or on a bike, when we hold an uneven load, or do anything unilateral like hold ourselves up in a pushup position, which people do a lot more often than they notice.

Some of these motions are very common causes of injury, so a lot of the exercises to train for them come out of the rehab world. Here is a short list—

> *Any of the rolling movements with heavier weight*
>
> *Half-Kneeling Presses*
>
> *Half-Kneeling Chops*
>
> *Half-Kneeling Lifts*
>
> *Rotational Rows*
>
> *One-Arm Bench Press*
>
> *One-Arm Pushups*

One-Arm Rows

One-Arm Presses

One-Arm Front Squat

Long Presses

As kids, soon as we are strong enough and stable enough, we start throwing things, like bowls of cereal across the room or keys into the toilet. As adults, once we're strong and stable enough from training rolls and twists, it's time to start chucking things around again. Medicine balls are a popular tool for this type of training, but you can throw anything that won't complain too loudly.

The goal of ballistic training is total force, which is the product of mass and acceleration. It's fine to throw a kettlebell, if you're strong and your downstairs neighbor isn't home, but throwing something smaller like a medicine ball or even a six-pack of coke will probably be more beneficial for training ballistics.

Here are a few ballistic throwing exercises, some of which don't even involve letting go of the object—

Overhand throws

Underhand throws

Throws with a step

Standing Side Twists

The Grappler

Dumbbell Snatches

One-Arm Kettlebell Swings

One-Arm Kettlebell Snatches

As you can see, there are a lot of ways to train the throwing pattern. Start on the ground and just roll around. Seriously, it feels so good you'll get hooked—which is a good thing because like the other five human movements, throwing, meaning rolling and twisting, is something you should practice Every. Damn. Day.

~Stevo Ledbetter

From the Ground Up

Once you go down the road of the sixth move, you can really branch out a lot of directions. This is why playing games is so good for fitness—you do all human movements in an unstructured, dynamic way and have a boatload of fun doing it. Honestly, if most adults started playing every day after work, I'd be out of a job!

But, they don't.

This keeps my career alive!

By the way, the fundamental human movements are knitted through Turkish getup work. This is one of the reasons Pavel and others insist that a program of just swings and getups can be an optimal workout.

Push

The getup is basically a moving one-handed plank. Both arms, the one on the ground and the one loaded, spin under load throughout the movement, but are constantly under load.

Pull

Perhaps a bit harder to see, the pivoting plank of the shoulder needs proper pulling dynamics.

Hinge

When you transfer through the positions from one-handed support to the hand off the ground, it's best to hinge. In fact, it is a good movement to practice by itself.

Squat

After rolling to the hand, the rest of the getup is a squat movement.

Loaded Carries

The TGU can be as difficult as any of the loaded carries for total body conditioning.

Tim, Stevo and I all agree that things begin *from the ground up*. From there, we can layer movement upon movement until we are leaping around, sprinting and throwing balls to one another. So, yes, the whole family of the sixth movements are important and crucial. And, most important, they're fun.

Ninth Question:
Are you willing to correct your problems?

ONE OF THE GREAT INSIGHTS I owe to Pavel is his understanding of time in an athlete's life. While it is absolutely true for most athletes that strength training and technique are in a yin and yang relationship, the amount of time given to these two qualities each week *isn't 50/50.*

I missed this insight over and over, until it finally stuck to the wall. I, too, need to pay attention here.

- ♦ Improving strength should help an athlete.
- ♦ Improving technique should help an athlete.
- ♦ Improving both strength and technique should really help an athlete!

So, the time spent in training for an athlete in a sport should not be divided 50/50 (half the time lifting and half the time working technique); rather it should be in a relationship perhaps like this—

- ♦ 80% of the time allotted on the sport
- ♦ 10% of the time allotted on strength training
- ♦ 10% of the time allotted on correctives

If you are going to train 10 hours a week, two hours a week will be doing the fundamental human movements and the mobility and movement correctives, and eight hours will be spent on your sport.

This idea works well with fat loss, too. The bulk of your time in a fat-loss pursuit should be in shopping, preparing and cooking your meals. Your energy should be addressing proactive strikes against the onslaughts of birthday cake, comfort food and "just a handful" of yummy, crummy treats. Your strength training will build some lean body mass, and your corrective work will make you feel better…so you move better…so you'll move more.

As an athlete, go do your sport and let your training support it. Everybody else should move around, cook good meals and live a good life. Then, come to the gym a bit each week and we'll kick-start your machine and realign the wheels.

Let's talk about applying this concept.

Elite athletes can train in the weightroom up to 10 hours a week, but that means the actual athletic training could be upwards of 40 hours a week including films, games and all the rest—and, all the rest can be a lot of time for a professional athlete. Imagine packing, dressing, showering and eating for the 162 games (not including exhibitions) that a major league baseball player has to do each year.

One way I address keeping my athletes motivated for both training their personal weaknesses and addressing corrective work is this: The first half of every training session is devoted to the perceived strengths in the five fundamental human movements. To this time devoted to their strengths, I add their mobility and flexibility correctives. It's an aspect of human nature I've come to acknowledge: If I reward you with what you do well, you'll do the little things like correctives.

Generally, this means my athletes will spend half their time working in the weightroom on what they do best. Usually, this means push and pull movements. But between sets of bench presses, for example, I have them foam roll, work on rolling movements or practice goblet squats. So you might see a set of a heavy set of five in the bench press, followed by the athlete foam rolling the hips and doing a few goblet squats. The five-minute rest period is filled with light corrective movements. We follow this up with the next set of five in the bench and another round of corrective work.

The other half of the training time is dedicated to weaknesses or omissions. Since you may be learning some new skills and movements, all energy has to be devoted to mastering the new tasks. I remember well learning to squat deep with Dick Notmeyer, when every set and rep was stressful physically, mentally and emotionally. It flat out hurt!

Some movements, like the warmup movements of goblet squat, swing and getup, also serve as correctives for many people. If you're learning the squat, a set of goblet squats between a set of military presses is quite instructive. It develops the pattern, certainly, but it also provides some extra time to master the movement. If you give this an honest try, you'll be amazed at the simplicity of this game-changing tweak.

Correctives can be those kettlebell moves labeled as warmups, but also include any specialized mobility work like we those find in the Functional Movement System's library of movements. These can include foam rolling and general flexibility work, too. Instead of resting between sets, you're actively battling your issues.

The time doesn't always work perfectly, as advanced athletes often have few weaknesses in the weightroom. But almost universally, they ignore loaded carries and struggle with squat depth. Finishing a workout with squats and a farmer walk or sled pushes is exhausting and there is no need to add anything between sets of car pushes.

The best way to look at your strengths and weaknesses is to grade them, like in school. As you'll understand when you think through this, I insist on a lousy GPA.

A—Give this to your real strength, your best movement. Yes, usually it's the push.

B—Obviously, this would be your second-best movement, but take some time to re-think about every three weeks. The loaded carry is often never done, and improves immediately.

C—Now, we're getting to the point where things become a little fuzzy. Some people have poor grades on three movements, but honesty is good here.

D—Usually I tell people to circle 'squat' and move on, but there are exceptions (these are called good athletes).

F—Alas, we'll need to see your folks at the parent-teacher conference. If you don't do a move that's key to human performance, well, you fail.

Any time you work your failing grade, you get better. So, any training you do on it will improve you, and any time you do additional low-level work—for example, the goblet squats as correctives for squats—you'll get better. Correctives are more than foam rolling and little odd moves on a wall, although I see the importance of those, too, of course.

The first half of the workout you'll work on your strong points. As Mark Reifkind, pointed out—

Work on your weaknesses,
but compete with your strengths.

I have no issues with an athlete having imbalances in the training profile, but it's my job to force people to attempt to bring up their weak points, whatever up might mean in each circumstance. But, you must compete with your strengths.

Let us look at the most common example: You have a great push and pull, which isn't unusual. So, the first half-hour of training will be bench presses and cable rows in a kind of slow superset.

Oh, you love me!

I ask for five sets of five in the bench press, and match that with five sets of 10 in the cable row. I often have people train with a 1:2 ratio in volume for push and pull because so many people have ignored pulling for so long. Moreover, most of adults have issues with posture and shoulders. This helps.

I also ask for full five-minute rest periods between the sets!
But, it isn't actually rest—this is the time for correctives.

During each rest set, we strive to do all the foam rolling we need, especially on the areas highlighted by the mobility screen we did at the beginning of the program. We also do varieties of toe touches, flexibility moves for the hips and legs, some wall work for the shoulders and various, almost always painful, thoracic mobility work.

From my experience, the correctives cause more sweating and exhaustion than the actual training. What is the upside of this method? You get the work in! I can't emphasize that enough.

Correctives can also be a few reps of the goblet squat, some rolling, getup drills or anything you need to address. Reward yourself with a lot of time on your strengths, but continue to hammer away at the areas that need to be addressed.

The rest of the training period is focused work on the weak movements. Let me tell you from the heart: A half-hour or more dedicated to early mastery of the swing and goblet squat is hellish, and ending with a basic farmer walk is exhausting. Within days of this kind of training, I get patted on the back as a miracle-worker—the client looks better, feels better and moves better.

What we're doing is targeting the issues and attacking them throughout the entire workout. Unlike most training programs that circle a 'do this' period each workout, we literally spend the whole time attacking issues. At the same time, we still keep the roots of lifts and movements that made you great...or whatever your level.

Soon, you'll be performing a few reps of the Turkish getup between sets of the strong movements. As you know, the getup is both an assessment and a corrective. In addition, it's an exhausting little exercise in its own right. But this can wait a few weeks until we have the basics of the getup and the movement patterns mastered.

Here's the strange thing: The loaded carries will not only expand your abilities quickly, but they're also mastered quickly. It isn't too long before we need to go through our assessments again.

In my life, I went from 'never squatted' to becoming a good squatter in just a few months. Later, when I discovered my 'F' grade on loaded carries, I addressed it swiftly. My greatest progress as an athlete happened, not surprisingly, when I brought up my squats and carries.

The take-away points—

Assess. Somehow, somewhere, please figure out where you are!

Never ignore your strengths, but combine your time working on your strong points, which is usually your favorite stuff anyway, with the mobility, flexibility or tissue quality work—the foam rolling and all of that.

When you work your weak points, keep all your energy focused there. Even at, or maybe especially at, the lowest introductory level, working a weak point is exhausting.

The idea of true conditioning work will radically change after doing loaded carries or squats for the unsquatted masses. Doing stuff you never do is exhausting.

Enjoy.

Chapter

Tenth Question:
Would you mind if everything was seamless from start to finish?

THE IDEA OF 'SEAMLESS' is an important concept in the way I teach, coach and attempt to live my life. At my funeral, I hope everyone is talking about the same person—in life, we call this integrity, the ability to be one person, the same person, in every situation.

As trainees, our efforts in every endeavor should be seamless, flowing from one situation or challenge to the next.

My method for making training seamless comes in several layers. First, I believe the mental focus for how the body should move can easily be labeled 'grace.' This is from the same tradition as calisthenics, a word that means, literally, 'beautiful strength.'

Second, it's really important for us to work with nature as she decides to fatten us up, weaken us and ties us into knots. A little knowledge can work wonders here, and the fastest route is to work with the body itself.

Depending on how you look at life, you could argue that we fight the constant fight against gravity our entire lives and it's inevitable we'll end up crushed and flattened. Or, like I advise, we can look at a more beautiful and simple approach. If you're truly interested in lifelong fitness, readjust your thinking to the beautiful and simple.

When we think of the way we age, or watch how many of us move, you might get the sense that something is missing.

I think you'll know what I am talking about when you watch an NBA game and then watch your neighbors play a pick-up game. Watch a master chef cut carrots and you'll see the same thing when you flail away with a knife. Keep your fingers out the soup, please.

Well, what is it?

It's grace. It's elegance. It's beauty.

It might sound odd, but if I were forced to talk about only one issue for those interested in fitness, it would simply be grace.

Before addressing the physical, simply decide to make the effort to be more elegant. Try to sit, stand and move smoother, with less jerks, pops and waddles.

When in doubt, try to keep your head calm and the top of your head pulled upward like it's being pulled by a rope. Yes, it's what you learned the first day of ballet, and it works for life, too.

The worst part of watching most fitness TV shows or internet videos is the quest for exhaustion. Form falls apart, the joints are stressed and we just get a sense of sweat and exhaustion. Honestly, it's better long term to strive for elegance and beauty and let the body adapt, well…beautifully.

We need to do this every day. Mastery in authentic movement should be the key for everyone, and consistent practice is the key to this idea. I have a concept I call 'the warmup *is* the workout' that addresses this need,

Here is the key: If something is important in exercise, it should be done every day. My warmup progressions reflect this insight. Although there's a lot of work here, one can add or subtract the intensity by changing the load or shortening the distance, time or repetitions. Please don't worry about the terms, as often names have little meaning save in context. Ludwig Wittgenstein, I owe you that one!

Not long ago, I was told the Tactical Frog is also called the Lion Pose, but then someone else said that 'this' is the Lion Pose, and then did a number of odd facial movements. Try to remember this: *Don't worry about the name, focus on the concept.*

For the past few years, I offered a weekly free workout at a local park, mostly to keep my coaching skills sharp. We do this warmup out there in the open air with just one kettlebell each—

> *Waiter walk with the non-dominant hand, then turn and return with it*
>
> *Repeat the walk with dominant hand*
>
> *Bottoms-up press walk as far as you can—with the 24K, I go nowhere! Again, switch hands and return.*

> *Goblet squat, get into the bottom position and then add a few curls*
>
> *Hip flexor stretch followed by a cross-body lower back stretch, then a variation of the windmill, pushing the heart to the sky*
>
> *Goblet squat*
>
> *Hip flexor stretch followed by a cross-body lower back stretch, then a variation of the windmill, pushing the heart to the sky*
>
> *Various wrist mobility moves*
>
> *Can-opener stretch, for the piriformis and QLs*
>
> *Tactical frog stretch*
>
> *Scap pushups , what we used to call horizontal shrugs*
>
> *Downward dog pose, and move through it*
>
> *Dolphin pose, and move through it*

To make every part harder, if you wish, do a set of 10 swings after each movement. If you want to go even harder, make it 20!

The idea of this warmup is to move through all the basic human movements, to lube the joints with strength exercises, mobility and flexibility movements, and to challenge the cardio-vascular system a little. It's a method that addresses the 'lean' part of lean body mass, and provides an easy way to work joint mobility.

And that, my friend, is the overriding focus of the strength coach, to seamlessly support your goals.

Although I will address programs and programming shortly, know that it's possible to do this kind of warmup five days a week. From there, you can pick a movement and train it with more focus.

As an example—

Monday
Warmup
Push

Tuesday
Warmup
Pull

Wednesday
Warmup
Hinge

Friday
Warmup
Squat

Saturday
Warmup
Loaded Carry

You need to do the fundamental movements as often as you can, but loading them can be done as seldom as once a week. Or less, really.

It is important not to think about these as exercises. They're movements. You don't have a walking day and an 'I-think-I'll-get-out-of-bed-today' day. No! You get out of bed, you walk around, you move every day!

A quick but crucial point: It might sound like I'm telling everyone to train hard every day. Honestly, I think the fundamental human movements should or could be daily, but life has a way of getting in front of this kind of thinking. Depending on your goals, this approach—the whole Intervention program—can be as little as two days a week to two or more sessions a day. For most of us, I suggest three training sessions a week and several simple movement sessions. Hey, just go take the dog for a walk, if that's what you have to do.

A strength coach should seek to seamlessly integrate the basics of human movement into training towards their clients' goals. The load may change. The volume may change. Movement, however, trumps everything else.

Training with the Triads and the Olympic Lifts

In *Intervention,* the concept of 'advanced' is just a little different. It doesn't mean NFL or Olympian. It means you have mastered the patterns, the grinds and symmetry of the movements. In addition, you're looking to accelerate your goals by adding a little pop to your workouts.

Keep this in mind: Many of the athletes I work with in Quadrant Two—as you remember, the collision sports and occupations—basically just do pattern work and grinds. For conditioning, we do things like The Eagle, seen on page 227, and variations of the ButtBurner 4000 from page 228. Often, due to injuries caused by all the collisions, Quadrant Two athletes can't do ballistic work in training because of symmetry issues.

So, why should you do the advanced work if the pros aren't doing it? These movements are seamless integrations of multiple human movements. I challenge you to perform a Litvinov or bodyweight snatch and tell me which of the five human movements—actually, five plus one!—it is. These movements are challenging in their demand for mastery across the spectrum, as well as in grace in coordination of strength, mobility and all-out effort. Plus, they're fun, efficient for fat burning and challenge us under ballistics.

Some of these movements changed my life.

The Triads—Push Press, Swings and Litvinovs

If you have the patterns for push, pull and hinge *and* you can do them with some competence in slow strength movements *and* you don't have any symmetry issues, let's talk about getting the bar up a little faster.

If you one-arm press 110 pounds with your right hand and can't press 35 with your left, do I have to tell you you're not ready? If you can't hold a plank for 10 seconds, please don't think momentum is going to help you.

Someone once asked me why push presses and push jerks—explosive overhead movements—seemed to add shoulder mass in just a few days. My answer lacked science, but I repeat it again as a reminder, "Because you use heavier weights."

The upside of these movements is you're going to be flying the bar up. The downside? If you're not ready, you're going to be tossing big weights overhead. I'm not crazy: Be sure you have things all nailed down before you toss weights overhead. You could end up with your coffin nailed down if you don't take my simple advice. Rest in peace is not part of my recovery toolbox.

A quick principle lost in our modern weight world: You press with your eyes, but you jerk with your ears. Very simply, when pressing, and that includes bench, military and everything else you can think pressing, you watch the bar go up with your eyes. Squeeze the rep up and watch it all the way. For whatever reason, this works.

But, to quote Brian Oldfield, "You can't think through a ballistic movement."

When jerking weights, *listen for the feet.* In fact, I teach the overhead jerks as a controlled dip followed by making noise with the feet. The funny thing is, everybody, every time agrees this is an amazing addition to the toolkit. This trick gets monkey-brain out of the way and allows you to move your body in a smooth, efficient manner without ruining it by over-thinking.

This is true, of course, for every movement, including all of the throws and most team sports. Thinking can be hazardous to your success! The next time you're exhausted in front of 10-million viewers with no game time left on the clock and have to make two free throws to tie things up and send the game into overtime…go ahead and think about it. Good luck.

Push Press

The push press is simple. Standing tall, with the weight on your chest—the normal start position for overhead pressing—dip your legs in a controlled bend. Then, vigorously drive the bar using your whole body toward the finished press position. It's relatively easy to do, but take your time adding plates. There's an issue with your chin being in the way of the bar as you drive it up, and it takes a bit of practice to learn to pull your chin out of the way. I learned that one the hard way.

Swings

Although I discussed swings in the hinge section, let me remind you, you need to have the pull, hinge and squat patterns locked down without symmetry issues before adding the dynamic movement on top of things. Part of the reason women pick up the swing so quickly is that much of their training experience tends to be pull, hinge and squat, and many avoid the excessive pushing movements that seem to draw men.

Maybe. No matter what, it's a rare situation where men pick up the snappy, hinging swing faster than women.

The Litvinov Workout

Of all the articles I have ever written, the one about Sergei Litvinov has received more criticism than anything I have done. The story in brief: former discus world-record-holder John Powell told me that in 1983 he saw the 196-pound Litvinov do a workout.

It was simple—eight reps in the front squat with 180 kilos (396 pounds) followed by a 75-second run around the 400-meter track. John reported that Litvinov did this three times.

Let's review the basics here. One, if you can front squat 400 for three sets of eight, you probably don't need a ton more advice from me. Two, those of you who don't think Litvinov actually did this, fine, but question John about it, not me!

What the earlier article critics also missed was this: I developed the following Litvinov program for use by elite military forces. There was an issue with torn hamstrings when certain things happened in combat. Bodybuilding and jogging doesn't prep a human for the needs of sprinting in combat under load. So, the following programming comes from my experience working with these forces.

I will also say this: These workouts transformed me and my athletes as throwers and I have to thank John Powell and Sergei Litvinov for this great transformational workout!

Perform any big lift, then drop the bar (gently) and run. My charges and I have used the following lifts.

Cleans

Clean & Press

Clean & Jerk

Deadlift

Front Squat

Overhead Squat

Snatch

We've also used any and all variations of snatches and swings with kettlebells and dumbbells.

Over time, we discovered 400 meters was far too long a run for our needs. But if you really desire a fat-loss blast, by all means run 400 meters!

The devil is in the details with this workout. Back squats don't work because racking the weight and running away involves way too much care and planning. We also discovered that even our lightest racks were a hassle to pack into the bed of a pickup to haul to a place where we could combine the lifting and running.

Also, I hated having my bar, weights and rack outside in lousy weather, collecting rainwater and mud. And I got tired of burning my hands on the hot weights in the summer sun.

Some lifts don't work very well either—we tried other lifts, like military presses and one attempt with the bench press, but it seemed foolish—lots of work and set-up for not much of a return on the time and effort. The clean & jerk never seemed to work right either. The lift has to be simple and easy to push quickly with little mental effort.

The best lifts are—

+ Front Squat
+ Overhead Squat, if you're good at them
+ Snatch
+ Swings with kettlebells or dumbbells—but really rack up the reps; try doing more than 30

The LitviSprint

Soon, the Litvinov became re-imagined as the LitviSprint. As we played with lifts and distance, one day we found ourselves with a kettlebell and a hill. We soon discovered that the speed and intensity of the run had a bigger impact on the workout than did the lift itself.

Kettlebell swings followed by a hill sprint of 30 yards or so seemed to leave us burning oxygen for hours after the workout. Moreover, massive amounts of meat and analgesic liquids (beer) did little to revive us.

Once again, the most obvious lesson of my coaching life has been reinforced: The more intense your training, the better. Yep, you knew that. So did I. Why, then, don't we follow the rule?

A nice little spin-off benefit began to emerge from LitviSprints. When learning a lift—very often the overhead squat—doing the sprint after the lift seems to speed up the learning process.

Why? I have two ideas.

1. When most people try to learn a new skill, they think too much. Like the late Joe Mills used to say: "Don't think! You're ill-equipped!

I'll try to teach the snatch or clean at a clinic and the questions just keep coming.

"Where do I put my thumbs?"
(Um, near your fingers.)
"Where do I put my elbows?"
(Between the upper and lower arm.)

In making the new lift even more complex by adding sprints, the questions stop, and we get after the movement. By magic, it looks okay.

2. People attempt perfection with a new skill the first time they try it. I've probably squatted near 100,000 reps and I still learn new things each time I work with Dave Turner or Bill Witt. This isn't going to happen on the first set! The challenge of sprinting seems to get us to forget perfection and focus on completion.

LitviSleds

Not content with leaving well enough alone, I began experimenting with LitviSleds. We do have some equipment issues here. Beyond the bar or kettlebell or dumbbell and the need for an area to run, you'll also need a sled and a harness.

Choose the lift you'll be performing before the sled drag. I cut our list down to these simple moves—

Front Squats

Overhead Squats

Swings with a kettlebell

The reason you have to simplify is that you hook yourself into the harness before you lift. You're hooked to the sled during the lift so you can drop the bar and sprint or drag away.

A caveat: Lift to the side of the path of the sled. Obvious, yes, but more than a few people have started the sprint or drag, snagged the weights and got yanked to the ground. It's funny to watch, but it may also really hurt. I'll still laugh, but you'll be hurt.

I have no idea how much you should load on the sled. I've found hooking a 70-pound kettlebell so it drags is about right for most people. The drag is nice, but don't overdo it like many, who think you need to pull a building. What's important isn't wallowing around like a pig in slop, but flying away like an athlete.

So, less wallow, more speed.

I also encourage you to go for about five seconds and not worry about distance. Otherwise, you lose the quality of effort almost immediately.

Litvinovs, LitviSprints and LitviSleds are based on a very simple idea. The quality of effort is far more important than the quantity—a concept you'll probably miss at first.

You may find this the fastest workout you've ever done. Don't be surprised if the workout seems too light or too easy. Judge the workout on the last set, not the first.

1. Pick a lift you know. Hit eight good reps with it, then sprint away for five seconds. Rest and repeat this two more times.

2. The next time you try the workout, try another lift and maybe go a bit longer on the sprint.

3. Do this easy progression about twice a week. If you choose to make this your whole leg workout, you've chosen wisely. If you're preparing for an athletic competition, try to see if this workout carries over to your field of play.

4. Don't measure rest periods the first few workouts. Let yourself recover fully. As the weights go up in the lift and the sprint gets to around 10 to 20 seconds, try to zero in on three- to five-minute recoveries. You'll need it.

Oh, one final note. At the 1987 World Championships in Rome, noticeably leaner, faster and more muscular four years after he saw the first Litivinovs, John Powell took second place in the discus. He was 40 years old, which is ancient in track and field, and this accomplishment is still considered one of the most amazing feats in track and field history.

The Olympic Lifts

If, and is this a big if, you have the pattern, the grind, the symmetry, the ballistics *and* can demonstrate a push press or jerk and a swing and a Litvinov, I will welcome you to the racks of Olympic lifting. Now, I can teach a roomful of ninth-graders the basics of weightlifting, but with any other population, I wait on these two moves. If the push, pull, hinge and squat are all dialed in, the squat snatch and its relatives are appropriate. If loaded carries are solid, I also add the squat clean and jerk, and the rest of the family, to the training load.

For more information, I offer a free 97-page ebook at *www. danjohn.net/pdfs/bp.pdf,* and have several DVDs on the topic at *davedraper.com.*

It is a difficult thing to type out Olympic lifting instructions. These need to be, in the jargon of football coaching, learned deliberately.

Walk it

Talk it

Chalk it

It is well worth the time and effort to master the O lifts…if you need to do them.

The Secrets of the Toolkit

As I have given the basics of *Intervention* to my fellow coaches, a few reoccurring themes have emerged as they take back the key points to try them on themselves and their athletes. I refer to these as the secrets, in the same way 'buy low, sell high' is a secret.

This list represents a year or so of insights, follow up discussions and breakthroughs.

- Get stronger in the fundamental human movements.
- This is the Atkins Diet of lifting—by deliberately being imbalanced for a while in training, you balance the real imbalances.
- There is no punishment in doing patterns—learning and coming back to patterns is never wrong.

- It's okay to get gassed from patterns and grind movements.
- Symmetry workouts are undervalued for their metabolic hit.
- If you need explosive movements, check patterns, grinds and symmetry. Look at the triads.
- The 80/10/10 rule is a valuable tool. Spend the bulk of your time on what your goal is all about—throwing, cooking and eating.
- As you go on this path, make sure it expands you out—think about the spiral.
- The goal is to keep the goal, the goal! Focus on it, don't get caught up in a bunch of other things.

Remember the toolkit and put the following to memory—

Most people will be in Quadrant Three, so just because you can do everything, doesn't mean you should. If you're a trainer or coach, learn to push people to Quadrant Three. You may spend your life convincing people they're not elite Special Forces or NFL players.

Get stronger in the fundamental human movements.

This is so obvious you might miss this important point, so pay attention: Almost universally, getting stronger is going to help you with your goals. Enough is enough when it comes to strength, but most people never even get close to the low-hanging fruit of strength training.

I work with men who gasp at my suggestion to bench bodyweight for 15 since they've never seen anyone that strong. Trust me, there are plenty of strong people on the planet. For fat loss, getting stronger is like the one-stop shop for turning yourself into a fat-loss machine.

Get in the weightroom and strive to add plates or move the pin down or slide over to a heavier dumbbell. It is the simplest thing I can teach you.

This is the Atkins Diet of lifting—by deliberately being imbalanced for a while in training, you balance the real imbalances.

One of the things that made the most sense about the original Atkins Diet was the two-week induction program to completely remove every carbohydrate from the diet. The thinking was this: If I've been imbalanced with carbs, let's swing all the way to the opposite towards fat and protein to achieve that balance. It worked for many in his diet and it works in exercise.

There's a chance that for a few weeks, you will do lots of goblet squats, farmer walking and rolling on the ground. You may ignore some things from the normal way you usually do things. But this imbalance in one direction is going to balance things out. It also happens very quickly.

If you don't have an authentic squat pattern and you ignore your rhomboids, for example, it's going to catch up in sports and in the process of aging. My orthopedic surgeon told me that nothing makes him sadder than when the decision to perform hip replacement is based on being able to relieve oneself. Losing the squat pattern through disuse or disease can be addressed by either the trainer and the surgeon, depending on the severity.

Let's be a bit imbalanced for a few weeks to bring the glaring weaknesses up to some standard.

There is no punishment in doing patterns—learning and coming back to patterns is never wrong.

Many people consider the patterns—planks, batwings, HATs, goblet squats, farmer walks and basic rolling—to be beginner moves. True, we should teach these early and often, but advanced trainers often benefit more from the simple stuff than anything fancy I can dream up.

Pattern work can be fat burning. Pattern work can be correctives. Pattern work can make you stronger. Don't consider pattern work to be sinful, punishment, regressive or embarrassing. These moves might be the answer to your issues and questions.

It's okay to get gassed from pattern and grind movements.

I'm never sure how to handle people who just want to feel 'worked out.' I like to train people to be and do better. If your sport, or your ego, demands some workouts that curl you over, vomiting into a flower pot, you can get there with patterns and grinds. Front squats followed by a truck push for a mile will get you all you need no matter what your needs are today.

Patterns and grinds are where you want to light things up, not on the Olympic lifts.

Symmetry workouts are undervalued for their metabolic hit.

When I travel, I often use the hotel gym to one-arm work. What I find amazing is that symmetry work, like basic correctives, seems to wear me out as much as a tough workout. There is a great conversation going on right now about why this happens, but many fitness experts have been finding their fat-loss clients get leaner doing corrective work and symmetry movements as opposed to more common movements like treadmills or cycles. It's worth keeping an eye on in the future.

Moreover, as I learned from my multiple wrist surgeries, training a healthy limb seems to spark the rehab in the limb that is in a cast. It is bizarre, but true. My return to normal was half the time of a normal patient according to my doctor and he thinks that my insistence on continuing to train around the injury and sling was a major factor. The body is one piece, one marvelous piece, and perhaps symmetry training reminds us that you may have two limbs, but one heart and one brain. Ideally.

If an athlete needs explosive movements, check patterns, grinds and symmetry. Look at the triads.

If.

Don't ignore that 'if.' Throwers, collision athletes and jumpers might need to snatch and clean & jerk. Grandma probably doesn't. Take the time to really search and deal with gaps, asymmetries and poor movement patterns before tossing bodyweight overhead at an Olympic lifting meet. The injuries come fast and hard in the quick lifts.

Spend quality time mastering the push press, the swing and the Litvinov family. For many of us, these three will be enough to break through any physical barriers or limitations. The O lifts changed my career, but I was physically, mentally and emotionally ready for the challenge. I also had months to master the movements before I had to compete in my main sport, too.

You may not have the years it takes to walk up the path to explosive movements in the weightroom.

If you do, get going.

The 80/10/10 rule is a valuable tool. Spend the bulk of your time on what your goal is all about—throwing, cooking and eating

Time is the key here. If you have 40 hours a week to spend on your goal, we get to have you in the weightroom for four hours of lifting and four hours of corrective work. My math is fuzzy, but that looks like about eight hours. The rest of the time should be working on your goal.

For fat loss, you would spend 32 hours a week shopping, cooking, measuring, weighing, and proactively dealing with eating and food. If you are a thrower…throw! If you are a hurdler, hurdle! If you are a sprinter, sprint! If you are a jumper, jump!

Now I have given away all my secrets as a track coach too.

As you go on this path, make sure it expands you out— the spiral.

There are dozens of authors who have said this better, but here it is: Be wary of getting your goal and discovering it wasn't worth it. Proper goal-setting should include expanding your life in every quadrant. Remember, the word 'fit' comes from the Old Norse word 'to knit.' Your life is your tapestry and it should have a great pictures, rich colors and a tight weave.

As I used to tell my students, "Your life is your message!"

The goal is to keep the goal, the goal! Focus on it, don't get caught up in a bunch of other things.

Although this point seems to contradict the previous point, remember this: As Chris Long points out to me all the time, "When you're up to your butt in alligators, it's too late to ask why you drained the swamp."

The best thing a personal trainer, life coach or good friend can do for you is to keep reminding you about your goal.

Coach Stevo's Case Three

The client in this story is an older client who is very aware of Point A, but Point B has changed on him with age. He is seeking a place to aim for, even as he continues diligently marching forward. More importantly, even though he has the knowledge to answer all of the 10 questions, he's lost touch with the five principles of the *Intervention* toolkit and is ill-equipped to deal with the answers. His intervention might be as simple as reacquainting himself with the integrity of his own body.

Four years ago, when he was training for Mr. Greater-Midvale, he really had things dialed in. Sometimes he goes back and to read his training journals from those days just to look for clues.

> *Foam Roll, Stretch, Dynamic Warmup*
> *Back Squat, 5x5*
> *Superset—*
> *Leg Extension, 10x3*
> *Leg Curl, 10x3*
> *1 set each to failure*
> *Superset—*
> *Seated Calf Raise, 10x3*
> *Standing Calf Raise, 10x3*
> *1 set each to failure*

That was a good workout. He could never do that workout now, though—too hard on the knees. He mostly sticks to the sliding hip sled for his leg work. Sometimes he does lunges. But the treadmill is the only way he can really put in the time he needs to stay lean.

It's definitely harder after age 40, but what isn't? He knows he needs to keep putting the time in if he's going to stay fit. Or, he often jokes to his friends, he could let himself go and just be a bear. After 20 years of lifting iron, he just doesn't have that drive to really finish a set of burnouts. Intensity is a young man's game.

Maybe he got lost after he started writing his training logs after he worked out. Once he worked out for a whole hour and couldn't remember what he'd done. He guessed curls; it was Tuesday and Tuesday was usually biceps day. Maybe he needed a program or something. He'd done every program he could think of though, and he always had to modify them. He'd read a couple of fitness magazines later on the treadmill. Surely there was something new he could do—something to jumpstart some progress, get him going again.

But he always knew what he would find in there.

"Six weeks to bigger arms!" My arms are already big.

"Three exercises guaranteed to blast your QLs!" My what?

"419 reasons you're not getting results!" Oh no, there's 419 reasons!

None of these helped. He knows his way around the weightroom. He used to be really big and cut. He knows how he got there before, and he doesn't want that again. Now he wants something else. He just wants things to be easier. But things are just getting harder. What's he doing wrong?

Chapter 22

The Five Principles

WHEN LITTLE BILLY asks me how to make the varsity team, I'm going to answer that question by calling on some fundamental principles about the best way to get him bigger, faster and stronger. Over the previous bulk of this book, I have asked you a lot of questions, but you have only asked me one—

How do I get from here to there?

The answer to that question will rely on my five principles.

1. Strength training for lean body mass and joint mobility work trumps everything else.
2. Fundamental human movements are fundamental.
3. Standards and gaps must be constantly assessed.

4. The notion of park bench and bus bench workouts must be applied together throughout the training lifetime.
5. Constantly strive for mastery and grace.

I'll talk about each of these in depth, and in the following chapters you'll see why I answer the way I answer.

Principle 1
Strength training for lean body mass and joint mobility work trumps everything else.

How much time should you spend on hypertrophy and joint mobility? The answer is simple: all the time you can spare! If the goal is to live well enough as long as you can, don't overlook either one.

Whenever I work on a computer, I notice as I tire from sitting, there's an urge to get up, stretch my arms backwards in this magnificent yawn that makes me look like the Y in the song, *YMCA*. I need to stretch my hips and psoas, my pecs, my biceps—in fact, I need to stretch the whole core of my bent-over body.

Years ago, Dr. Vladmir Janda began discussing the muscles necessary for posture. To simplify, and that's always a slippery slope, he separated muscles into two groups: tonic, which tend to shorten when tired (or old!) and phasic, which tend to weaken under stress (or age, I dare say).

A simple chart—

Muscles that get tighter—Tonic	*Muscles that get weaker—Phasic*
Upper Trapezius	Rhomboids
Pectoralis Major	Mid-back

Biceps	Triceps
Pectoralis Minor	Gluteus Maximus
Psoas	Deep Abs
Piriformis	External Obliques
Hamstrings	Deltoids
Calf Muscles	

I usually explain it this way—

If a tiger chased you up a tree, the muscles you use to hang on to the branch for a long time are tonic muscles. If you decided to chase a deer to throw rocks at it, you'd use your phasic muscles.

Sadly, most trainers work this backwards. They tend to emphasize the mirror muscles like the pecs and biceps—with, say, bench press and curls—and ignore the muscles that are really the muscles of youth.

Using our fundamental human movements

Push: *Deltoids and Triceps*
Pull: *Rhomboids*
Hinge: *Butt*
Squat: *Butt*
Loaded Carries: *Butt*

Folks, the butt is the muscle of youth. Sit on that for a while.

When I first came to the world wide web, I had this wonderful conversation with some women in the 100-Pound Club. To be a member, one needed only to lose 100 pounds. Most of them had figured out the biggest bang for the buck in terms of weightlifting were the standing press and the squat. Looking at this list above and the two movements, you can see they intuitively understood the need for strengthening the phasic muscles.

Lifting weights can be a way to gain more lean body mass *and* provide some additional joint mobility. There's a basic assumption I make before training an athlete, or really anyone, and it comes in two parts.

First, movements tend to trump muscles. I do not believe in an arm day nor a leg day. I think 'basic human movement' day. Sure, we can break this work into vertical and horizontal and single-limb and probably many more options, but generally we need to deal with these each day, and certainly each training session.

Remember: *movements first.*

Principle 2
Fundamental human movements are fundamental.

I know this is an obvious point. Trust me, when I first started to train, I was told *fundamentals first.* Five decades later, the concept of fundamentals first hit me like a lightning bolt: *We need fundamentals first!*

Years ago, I met this gentleman who was a marriage therapist. He said something that made me think for a few months, "You know, adultery is hell on a marriage."

Then, he sort of caught himself and said, "Of course, something like this has been said before."

For the readers who missed his point, see the Sixth Commandment or the various writings of any religious tradition. But, the point here is important: after 15 or so years of work, with perhaps 300 clients—maybe more—and after, it seems, significant reflection, he came to a conclusion.

You will notice, too, that our marriage therapist didn't use statistics or numbers to prove his point. Covert Bailey, in his work *Fit or Fat?*, has that wonderful question, "If a supermarket had a sale of '10 pounds for a dollar,' would you buy it? No, wouldn't you first ask, '10 pounds of what?'

Always ask, '10 pounds of what?'"

The insight our marriage therapist provides is the concept of prolonged reflection. Take a moment here: I want you to think about point number two—

Fundamental human movements are fundamental.

The longer I coach and work with people, the more convinced I am that doing the basic movements trumps everything else. People want fancy machines, ornate programming and Captain Whizzbang's high tech monitoring equipment, but, honestly, the fundamental movements—the basic pushes, pulls, hinges, squats and carries—are going to be the foundation. You can make gains by using kettlebells, bars, rocks or weighted bags.

When I first met Dick Notmeyer, his givens were the Olympic lifts and the front squat. When I first met Ralph Maughan, his givens were full-turn throws, some lifting, and showing up consistently for one's whole career. Throughout every need fad and fashion, these givens have been proven correct over and over again.

But, that's the key: Like the insight from my marriage therapist friend, if you make an honest effort to explore your art, you're going to discover that the true gems are the things you probably learned the first day.

It's pretty simple, but it might take you 30 years to simplify things.

Principle 3
Standards and gaps must be constantly assessed.

I'm often confused when people ask me about standards. I get this surprising question: I can't do this standard. What should I do? I can easily do this or that one, but not this.

You know the answer: lack of focus, lack of doing the moving or just lack of motivation. If I could go back in time, I would sit down with myself circa a few decades ago and explain this truth—

> *You only move forward by vigilantly and aggressively sorting out your weaknesses and your gaps and bringing them up to some standard. True, compete with your strengths, but your ability to move ahead is all about dealing with your gaps.*

I did an interesting thing as a young athlete. At the end of each year, I wrote down a list of things to my future self (there is a lot of time travel in my thought processes), to tell him the clues to success for the next year. As I recently reviewed some of these, it was obvious I was trying to tell myself to do more hypertrophy work (bodybuilding), use more variety in general training especially movement, and giving warnings about trying to do too much too soon.

This book is dedicated to the warnings I failed to heed my whole career!

It's a tight rope walk. The strengths and interests and skills that propel one to elite levels cannot be ignored. For me, it was the speed and explosion gained from the Olympic lifts, and the tenacity to spend up to four hours a day throwing.

Then, my gaps showed up. I didn't do loaded carries; my squat movement had issues; and I needed smarter recovery methods to support the training load. I also needed to be in a locale more conducive to big discus throws.

My solution was to keep on O lifting, squatting with too much of a forward lean, and throwing harder and harder. What I needed was to fill in the gaps, not more work on my strengths.

This is why a smart trainer hires his own personal trainer. As the joke goes, any attorney who represents himself has an idiot for a client. The same goes for fitness professionals: If you coach yourself, your client has issues. That's why I hire a personal trainer to work with me at least once a week.

Buddy Walker, my trainer, makes me do the things I know I should do, but find reasons not to do these important things. Good training programs constantly come back to the notion that it's the gaps that will cause the problems over the long term.

Mike Boyle's insight about mobility—the image of the door and door frame and how the gaps must fit just right—gives us an insight about lifelong fitness. Mobility training has to be focused on keeping the gaps 'just right.' There's no great need for outrageous mobility or flexibility to live a normal life and even, usually, to be in elite sport. Sure, if you want to be in the circus and fit in a shoebox, you need more than I can offer. But, for the rest of us, once again, enough is enough.

Principle 4
The notion of park bench and bus bench workouts must be applied throughout the training lifetime.

There are thousands of books on the 'how' of fitness. I have books that promise fitness in 30 minutes a week, a few minutes a day, the conditioning of a convict, the fitness of an Olympian, and the body of a Spartan. I'm convinced most people know the 'how' of fitness.

If you had a competent physical education coach at any time in your life, you probably have the basics. Go jog two laps, knock off a few stretches and calisthenics and then go play a game for an hour. Report all injuries and be sure to shower and clean your feet because the scourge of athlete's foot is still a worry.

I was once told that the average amount of use of a home treadmill is 7.2 times. The rest of its life in your house will be to hold clothes and remind you of past attempts to achieve fitness.

The problem in our approach to fitness seems to lie in 'why am I doing this?' versus how. And, I know why you want to train—

To get into shape
To lose some weight—ideally fat
To look better, feel better and move better

You know how to do it and why to do it, but there sits that treadmill in the corner, covered in shirts, pants and towels.

I think the problem is this: The fitness industry only sells full-throttle, death-march, total-commitment training concepts. And, frankly, most of us simply can't do that day in and day out.

Perhaps we can learn a little lesson from those in the business of religion.

In the *Tale of Two Benches,* Archbishop George Niederauer, my former boss, describes sitting on a bus bench. When we wait for a bus, we're filled with expectations. The G bus should be here at 8:11. If I look up at 8:11 and don't see it, I begin to panic. At 8:13, my day is ruined. I want to get off this bench and get going somewhere else! The bus should be here now. Wait…now!

The park bench, however, is a time to sit and listen and watch. We wait for nothing. The local squirrels that showed up yesterday may or may not be here today. And, that's okay. We don't call the city squirrel police if they don't show up when we want them to show up.

The approach most athletes take to competition is the bus-bench idea. On Saturday the 26th, I will defeat all who show up, break all my personal records, find perfection in all I do, and meet the person of my dreams.

This, my friends, is the G bus of sports preparation and life. It's a tough model to follow. As I look over my nearly 50 years in organized competition, I can only think of a few times (three?) when the G bus showed up on schedule.

For most athletes most of the time, and for most of us for most of our lives, the park bench model is much more appropriate. When you compete or train, take time to enjoy the view, breathe the air, and don't worry about the squirrels! Whatever comes along during your competition or training should be viewed through the lens of wonder and thanks.

My great joy in competing in Highland Games has a lot to do with the friendships made, the variety of events and the party atmosphere. Highland Games athletes don't make fools of themselves complaining about a bad performance. The events make a fool of us!

To get a park-bench mentality, we have to realize that at best, very few competitions will be perfect. In addition, when the stars arrange for you to have those perfect competitions, you had better not try to mess it up with a lot of extra energy—you just have to let it go.

The park bench attitude also helps with the 20% of competitions where things all go wrong. If you can keep your wits and feed a squirrel or two, you may just salvage the competition!

By the way, nothing frightens your competition more than a serene smile on your face. They think you're up to something.

I fully believe life is a competition. There's just enough Darwin in me, as well as a Master's degree in History, to believe that our lives are tenuous at best, and survival, without any hint of irony, reflects on our fitness.

If your survival depends on your fitness, so why are you slamming your head against a wall to get it?

Train hard, but enjoy competition. Compete hard, but enjoy your training. One key final point must be kept in mind: *Never judge a workout or training program as good or bad solely on a single day.*

I often tell new throwers, "Sorry, you are just not good enough to be disappointed." Judging one's worth as an athlete over the results of single day is just idiocy, and will lead to long-term failure. Epictetus, the Roman Stoic philosopher tells us—

> *We must ever bear in mind that apart from the will, there's nothing good or bad, and that we must not try to anticipate or to direct events, but merely to accept them with intelligence.*

As an athlete, I took to heart a few pieces of insight from my study of religion. First, let things happen and don't judge them as good or bad. Enjoy the opportunity to train and compete.

Second, find yourself a community of people who support your goals, and be sure you support your goals, too. Don't lose sight of the spiral as you strive to achieve your goals.

The Bus Bench Workout

What would be an example of a bus bench workout? To be honest, it's the kind of thing most people want. Call it a program, a cookie-cutter approach or a training manual, but it's that long page after page after page of 'do this' and 'do that' most people want to have in their hands.

When an aspiring freshman college football player comes into the weightroom the day after he gets his first program from his college strength coach, he loves to rush over and show me this secret workout. Usually, it's just slapped together from this place and that article, and has lots and lots of things to do. And, it can work.

Hey, another thing: I loved the Velocity Diet. I am not recommending it to you, but I loved it. It's the ultimate bus-bench approach to dieting and exercise. Here you go, for review—

For 28 days, you'll eat six very low-carb protein shakes.

Oh, and one day a week, you get to eat a single solid-food meal. Be sure to cut back on the shakes that day!

That's right, four solid meals in a month.

Friends, if you don't lose bodyfat on the V Diet, you have by all rights and all considerations the authority to scream and shake your fist as wildly and as angrily as you wish. If you honestly followed the program for 28 days and didn't lose bodyfat, you have issues I'm not sure I can address. Complain away!

I have done bus bench programs that have names like—

Bigger Biceps in Two Weeks
Two Weeks to a Firmer Fanny
Soviet Squat in Six Weeks Program

And the list goes on and on.

Generally, bus bench programs have built-in durations like two weeks or 12 weeks and, if you follow the directions, you should be changed in that time. If not, the program *failed*.

Again, complain away.

Everyone should have about two bus bench programs a year. Clarence Bass, a bodybuilder noted for his lean physique and who's known as Mr. Ripped, continues to schedule an annual photo shoot to give him a focus each year to, well, get on the bus. After age 70, it's still working well for him. Many people use January and the weeks leading up to bikini season times to refocus. I applaud the effort.

The issue I have is that most people turn all 52 weeks of the year into the bus bench mentality. The internet forums rage about how whatever is latest and greatest is the right answer. The cliché in sports is this: The best thing is the thing you're not doing.

Open one of your deep, dark cupboards and look at the miracle pills, goos and patches that were touted as the answer to all your problems. I have survived high carb, low carb, high fat, low fat, high protein and low protein diets, only to learn that most diets are simply the bus bench mentality at play. And please listen, this is important: *Two weeks on any diet works miracles for people.*

"It worked so well, I stopped doing it."

Here's the thing to remember. If you honestly tried limiting yourself to 500 calories and an injection of beef plasma every day for a few weeks and failed to achieve your goals, blame the program! If it was a success, refocus for a while, readjust your priorities, but don't celebrate with two-dozen doughnuts. One dozen is plenty!

I can't emphasize this enough. The bus bench approach to training and diet is *right*. It's absolutely right about twice a year.

Like the old joke about a broken clock, a broken clock is right twice a day; a focused, disciplined attack on a goal is a great thing to do.

Just not all the time!

To continue just a step farther, the bus bench mentality is sadly destroying education in America. Many parents are convinced there's a straight line, a cause-and-effect relationship between, for example, membership in a club sport leading to a Division One athletic scholarship, or an A in Advanced Placement Biology leading to medical school.

Education and fitness are both served by a healthy mix of bus-bench and park-bench mentality. I'm convinced the bulk of our time should be spent doing park bench work. Children should read for pleasure and enjoy good books. Certainly they should be challenged with rigorous questions concerning some books, and their lives will be enriched by a deeper understanding of the books they read and enjoy.

Don't forget to enjoy.

Principle 5
Constantly strive for mastery and grace.

Everything I know about mastery can be found in the work of George Leonard. When his *Esquire* magazine article called "Ultimate Fitness" came out in the 1980s, he highlighted the idea that everything we learn in sports and business should also lead us to the same insights about life. I have spent the past few decades merely nodding in agreement to everything Leonard noted in that article and later in his book, *Mastery.*

The lessons learned about preparing, peaking and programming for victory in the ring or on the field are lessons of life. Sometimes you can get away with cutting corners, but usually you can't. But, like love and life, I have often noted that the best performances have a silken easiness to them that defies explanation. For me, true mastery is so graceful and grace-filled that someone who is unaware of what is optimal will still appreciate the moment.

I made some points about grace in the Seamless section, the 10th question beginning on page 171, but be sure to remember this: *Always strive for a quiet head, efficient movements and sense of calm while training.*

True, it is difficult to look elegant with sweat burning your eyes, but try.

I think proper fitness training will be seen in the body shape of the person training correctly. Not only will we move gracefully—masterfully—when in shape, but there will be a beauty in the form, too.

Art DeVany brought this to my attention when I first logged onto the internet. He noted that the X look for men is a sign of health. Men, he noted, should have broad shoulders, a thin waist, powerful buttocks and thighs, and should not worry about showy arms. Women, on the other hand, show fertility with an hour-glass figure, a narrow waist bordered by a rounder top and bottom.

Images of Raquel Welch in *One Million, BC* can fire an immediate response in most men. It still works for me.

The X look and the hour-glass figure also have a subtle aspect many people miss. My years of overtraining my strength led me to lots of physical trauma. To undo those years of damage, and this is not hyperbole as we're talking about literally decades of poor exercise choices and poor posture, I learned the two keys to a better physique, better performance and happy, pain-free joints.

And, you may well ask, what are the two keys? *Grace and compression.*

Now, grace might be apparent to most people, and because of that sadly ignored, but compression is another issue altogether.

Not long ago, I had one of those moments that provided clarity for life. I attended a late night hot yoga session and discovered the harder I pulled myself into a position, the more my body responded by expanding in the rest period. Literally, what we compress, expands.

Certain areas of the body seem to work best after compression. There have been some new axioms in the fitness industry in the past few years—certain joints and areas needing flexibility and others needing mobility. It does seem, too, that compression helps some areas open up to flexibility and mobility.

The martial arts traditions of pressurized stretches to open the feet and wrists are an example, as are the scap pushups people do in training. These are basically pushups where the arms never bend, but the upper body relaxes and drops through the shoulder. That refreshing crack in the upper back usually indicates you got it right. The bottom position of the goblet squat, and various moves like curls in the bottom position actually open up the body by pushing—compressing—it apart.

It's funny, but often in training after we do a series of compressions, I notice people standing up with what I call either the Yul Brenner or the Peter Pan stance. For the mental image, think of Yul in the *King and I* or the cocky hands-on-hips stance of Peter when he deals with Captain Hook. You might find yourself doing it!

Grace and compression should live in a yin and yang relationship in your fitness goals. When standing for long periods, walking and sprinting, and for the movements of your training, strive for grace as the key quality in your efforts.

In restorative work and mobility work, let yourself dance through the compression and expansion feeling, and be sure not to let either partner lead.

Grace is a remarkable thing. I was going to say amazing, but, well…

If you make the conscious decision to sit more gracefully, you tend to rise more gracefully. On an odd note, if you decide to throw the discus more gracefully, with a calm elongated head and quiet movements, the discus will thank you by flying farther. There's an elegance in superior sport and artistic movements that even someone completely unfamiliar with the performance will usually know who's the best without having to resort to the box scores.

Beautiful movement is not only a joy to watch, but it tends to be pain-free. As Bill Witt notes about throwing: Good technique shouldn't hurt. If you do something 10,000 times a year, like Witt encourages, it can't be 10,000 painful reps.

To get the benefits of compression, you can take a yoga class, join a mobility group, or take a deep study into flexibility. Traditional stretching movements are very important in understanding the role of compression. Literally, we squeeze ourselves into positions, then relax and expand.

Pavel has a wonderful book, *Relax into Stretch,* where he outlines techniques such as waiting out the stretch, proprioceptive neuromuscular facilitation (PNF), isometric stretching, contrast breathing, forced relaxation and, my favorite, the Clasped Knife Technique. Somehow, comparing stretching to the use of a switchblade awakens something in my interest in learning to stretch at a higher level.

How much time and effort should you spend in these efforts? As you age, besides not getting into a serious traumatic accident, there are two things to focus on—increasing lean body mass and maintaining joint mobility.

It's not the first time I've said this.

Implementing the Intervention Program

Understanding Repetitions before Programming

I have spent my life trying to understand weightlifting. It seems to me there are three important keys.

Fundamental Human Movements
Reps and Sets
Load

This is the correct order we should approach weightlifting. We need to establish the correct postures and patterns, then work around reasonable numbers of movements in a training session and, finally, we should discuss the load.

Sadly, the lifting population—and I am guilty of this too—has switched the order and made a 500-pound deadlift the answer to improving one's game or cutting some fat. There is some truth in this, but we can all agree that quality of movement is both safer short- and long-term to the individual.

And note well, I said "training session" in the paragraph above. If you buy into the concept of training the fundamental human movements, stressing posture, patterns and grace, you have to realize that training sessions are about more than just breathing hard, sweating or vomiting.

Oh, I can work you out. Just run back and forth for a couple of hours every time I blow a whistle. But, please don't think that's going to improve your skill set or your long-term ability to do anything from sport to aging gracefully.

I like to teach those key patterns of human movement with these three basic kettlebell moves: the swing, the goblet squat and the getup. The hip displacement continuum unlocks the secret that hip movement has two ends, the swing and the goblet squat. The swing demands maximal hip hinge and minimal knee bend while the goblet squat demands maximal hip hinge along with maximal knee bend. The getup is a one-stop course in the basics of every human movement from rolling and hinging to lunging and locking out.

With these three moves as a base, add the pushup and honestly, you might be done. Let me say this: Get the basic patterns and movements into a program with the least amount of teaching, learning and failure you can maintain. 'Less is more' is bigger than a buzzword when it comes to addressing the issues of lean body mass and joint mobility.

I believe three simple things about training sessions—

1. Training sessions need to be repeatable.
2. Training sessions should put you on the path of progress towards your goals. I still can't believe I have to tell people this.
3. Training sessions should focus on quality.

Memorize this list!

Now, to apply these points to strength training workouts, I have found that keeping an eye on the correct number of repetitions in any given workout is the easiest way to insure that quality movements are balanced with appropriate loads.

Whole Body Movements and the Rule of 10

Rule of 10: The total number of quality reps is 10 or fewer. Less is more here.

The Turkish Getup

Snatch

Clean and Jerk

Deadlift

For elite athletes, squat variations with a barbell

I discovered, as many have, that around 10 reps in a workout is the right number for whole body lifts for an experienced lifter. This rule of 10 means you have probably 10 real reps in a workout with a big lift like the deadlift, the snatch and the clean and jerk.

In teaching the getup, or using this wonderful lift as a tool to discover your body, keep the reps around 10. You can think about this as a total of 10 with five on the right and five on the left, or you can try 10 right and 10 left. But…really?

If I do getups as part of my warmup along with some getup drills for this or that (the highly technical name I use for correctives), I am sweating and pushing into a workout around 10 total reps.

Certainly, at times you can do more. Recently, we had a wonderful challenge of doing one rep on the first of the month and adding a rep a day up until the 31st. At the end of the challenge, one guy told me he was doing this right *and left*! That's 62 getups!

That's a good challenge, but perhaps not a training program.

Week in and week out, think around 10 reps per training session for the getup.

This also works well with the big lifts—the clean, snatch and deadlift. Moreover, I have discovered that even movements from the family tree of pushes and pulls work well in this rep-range.

Most experienced lifters would recognize these kinds of workouts—

Three sets of three

Five sets of two

Two sets of five

Five-three-two

Six to 10 singles

The fundamental human movements can be used well with the Rule of 10. I don't suggest, unless you are a Silverback Gorilla, for you to do all five (plus one) movements heavy and hard with the rule of 10 for a daily workout.

Some suggestions for the Rule of 10 and the basic movements—

- ♦ **Push:** *Bench Press, Incline Press and Military Press with a barbell*
- ♦ **Pull:** *Rows with a barbell*
- ♦ **Hinge:** *Deadlift, Deadlift Variations, Cleans, Snatches with a barbells*
- ♦ **Squats:** *Front Squats or Back Squats with a barbells*
- ♦ **Loaded Carries:** *Farmer Walks, Prowlers, Car Pushes— heavy loads and short durations*

Picking a rule-of-10 lift and going heavy on the basics is very possible, but you need to build in some easy days and cycle the load. Simple strength is an attempt to do this and I will be expanding on this in Chapter 25, beginning on page 233.

If attempting to do a workout with nothing but the rule of 10, be sure a few of the movements are relatively light and easy. I usually refer to this as tonic, something that refreshes. Consider the batwing, goblet squat or other corrective movements as part of this program.

By the way, I've had people report great success with the rule of 10, multiple workouts a week and kettlebells. The focus is on—

Heavy Single-Overhead Presses (Left and Right)

Loaded Pullups (Pullups with kettlebell dangling from the waist)

Loaded Pistols (Hold a kettlebell, both left and right legs)

Heavy Getups

Although this is beyond the scope of this book—if you can do these movements with a half-bodyweight kettlebell or more, you don't need *Intervention,* for now—it's an interesting experiment with the human body. The chief complaint is the workouts take so little time and the feeling of 'not doing anything' is hard to overcome.

One final point: I note that these are whole-body lifts. These movements require an orchestration of the body in a way that's unusually taxing. Often people ask me if the bench press is truly a whole-body exercise and I remind them of my core belief: *The body is one piece.* Under a heavy bench press, say 500 pounds, you will discover that if I stick a fork in your calf, it will distress your performance. In fact, it might be the direct cause of your death.

Moreover, these movements, done under large loads, will quickly exhaust your reserves. Keep the reps down on the big movements.

The Bodybuilding Movements (Half-Body Moves)

15–25 Total Reps for the Movement
Somewhere between 15 and 25 reps is the right rep-range for working the grinding movements. From my recent experiences, the basic moves, including nearly all the presses, are best done in this range. Again, if you are benching 600 and military pressing 300 or 400 pounds, refer to the rule of 10.

For one thing, it's a reasonable workout. Three sets of five, for example, ends up being what most people actually do on the 5x5 workouts and variations. That's a lot of serious front squats if you aren't counting warmups.

The whole issue of volume always needs to be addressed. Certainly, we've done those contests where you bench 100 pounds

100 times just to one-up a friend, but that isn't really a training program; that's just fun.

Keep having fun, but plan things occasionally, too.

The goblet squat seems be perfect around 15–25 reps per workout. I offer you the humane burpee as a way to try this concept—

> *10 Swings*
>
> *5 Goblet Squats—put the kettlebell down between your feet, under control*
>
> *Inchworm out to the pushup position—walk on your hands*
>
> *5 Pushups*
>
> *Inchworm back to the start*
>
> *10 Swings*
>
> *4 Goblet Squats—put the kettlebell down between your feet, under control*
>
> *Inchworm out to the pushup position—walk on your hands*
>
> *4 Pushups*
>
> *Inchworm back to the start*
>
> *10 Swings*
>
> *3 Goblet Squats—put the kettlebell down between your feet, under control*
>
> *Inchworm out to the pushup position—walk on your hands*
>
> *3 Pushups*
>
> *Inchworm back to the start*
>
> *10 Swings*

> *2 Goblet Squats—put the kettlebell down between your feet, under control*
>
> *Inchworm out to the pushup position—walk on your hands*
>
> *2 Pushups*
>
> *Inchworm back to the start*
>
> *10 Swings*
>
> *1 Goblet Squat—put the kettlebell down between your feet, under control*
>
> *Inchworm out to the pushup position—walk on your hands*
>
> *1 Pushup*
>
> *Inchworm back to the start*
>
> *Finished!*

That's 50 swings, 15 goblet squats and 15 pushups. Eight, five and two counts will give you the same results with fewer swings if you need that (only 30!).

Most of us recognize this range as the bodybuilding workout. Reg Park famously wrote of the 5x5 workout for nearly every bodypart with rather heavy loads. He claimed this built both size and power, and he had the results to show for it.

The key to 15–25 reps is finding the right load for the movement. There's a simple formula here:

If you can't do 15 (three sets of five, five sets of three), the load is too heavy.

If 25 reps are a breeze (five sets of five), the load is too light.

And, yes, people pay me money to explain this to them.

Fundamental human movements in this range reflect more of a traditional bodybuilding approach to strength training.

Push

Most gyms have a variety of machines for pushing, including the standard varieties of bench, inclines, declines, militaries and the like. Of course, the barbell variations work well here.

Pull

Again, there are dozens of pulling machines available, and certainly the barbell will work well here, also.

Hinges

These can be a bit tricky in some gyms as often the quick lifts, deadlifts and the like are banned. Which makes one wonder why they are called gyms! The trap bar has become a popular variation for many, although it tends to make some people squat-hinge.

Squats

Please don't include leg extensions, leg curls, innie and outie machines and leg presses as squat workouts. For the typical lifter, squat variations of five by five is a great workout.

Loaded Carries

Many of the loaded carries support a bulk-and-power approach to training. Oddly, bag carries seem to do a lot to build that human inner tube so necessary for building a solid foundation.

Patterns and The Explosive Kettlebell Lifts

The total number of reps can be quite high, 75–250, but insist on quality of movement.

A few years ago, I picked up this idea of doing 20 swings with one kettlebell and 10 swings with two. After doing literally hundreds of swings a day, I noticed my technique held up fine in that 10- and 20-range. This is the basic teaching of sports: *Don't let quantity influence quality.*

In other words, 10 good reps is far better than dozens of crappy ones. If you want more volume, do more sets.

Absolutely, there are times when you should do more than 20. There are times when you want to do all kinds of things. There are times, though (known as most of the time), where you just keep moving ahead. I usually call these 'punch the clock' workouts and I think it's the key to staying in the game.

So, you may ask, is this enough?

Over time...yes!

Yes, you can do more, but you want to be able to do it day in, day out—literally year in and year out.

Higher-rep work has great value, yes, *but keep the quality of work high.* The fundamental human movements and the higher-rep work need a bit of work.

Push

The plank is an ideal long push. Stu McGill's insight of 120 seconds of planking also gives us a target of how the reps should fit into this range.

Pull

Batwings are an interesting way to move into higher reps. Again, like the plank, this is a time issue, but many have discovered that the isometric work of the batwing is best served with longer holds after an appropriate break-in period.

Hinges

Of course, the kettlebell swing and snatch are the top of the pyramid for high-rep work in hinging. If your technique is solid, there's some value in moving to higher reps, obviously.

Squats

High-rep squats are not always a good idea unless you have the movement mastered. If you have the courage to do high-rep goblet squats, up to 50, give it a try. Keep the next day a bit open.

Loaded Carries

Basically, when you add it all up, a total of 120 seconds of loaded carries would be a long day.

Be sure to have movements locked down before trying to explore higher reps.

Load is often the problem for most people. To completely stereotype the entire population of the planet, men tend to go too heavy and women tend to go too light. The standards of the fundamental human movements are appropriate targets, but sometimes training sessions should be about the movements. Load is the tough one, to be honest.

I argue this: If you have a beautiful, graceful, smooth movement and you are in the right rep- and set-scheme, you can determine you're using the right load by noting—

- If you had the load right, you got the reps and sets as planned.
- If you didn't get the reps and sets, it was too heavy. Adjust.
- If you found the reps and sets too easy, it was too light. Adjust.

You may need to adjust the load often. I find that one of the first signs of overtraining is when I start to struggle with what had been a reasonable weight on the bar. It's so simple, most people miss it.

Programming with Patterns and Grinds:
The Four Steps

As NOTED BEFORE, in terms of popularity the five basic human movements from are in this order—

+ Push
+ Pull
+ Hinge
+ Squat
+ Loaded Carry

However, in terms of impact—the ability to be a game-changer—we need to reverse the order—

+ Loaded Carry
+ Squat

- ◆ Hinge
- ◆ Pull
- ◆ Push

The five movements have an interesting relationship when we move into the area of metabolic conditioning. I first heard the term 'metabolic conditioning' in the late 1970s or early '80s through the work of Ellington Darden.

Essentially, metabolic conditioning is that odd feeling when moving from one movement, say squats, to another movement like a pullup. Even though the heart rate is within reason—cardiovascular conditioning, so to speak—and the muscles about to be used are fresh, so strength endurance isn't an issue, the athlete can't gear up enough 'whatever' to do the job.

Don't go crazy with metabolic conditioning. Yes, it has a value. Yes, it's a finisher or a gasser, but it can also lead to a variety of issues like joint problems from crappy reps to the serious medical conditions that seem to be sweeping some facilities.

The important thing is the mix when training metabolic conditioning. Patterning movements work well here because the amount of movement error is minimal. Patterning work is often isometric—and it's difficult to mess up a movement that isn't moving.

Patterning movements work well with grinds. However, they don't all work well together! Oh, sure, you can slap together anything, but the following four combinations are ideal for most people.

Combo One
The Pattern Movement of Loaded Carries, Mixed with the Grind of the Squat

A few years ago, I discovered the combination I call The Eagle. The school mascot where I was teaching at the time was the Soaring Eagle, so the name was a natural. It combined the simplest of the loaded carries—the patterning movement of the farmer walk—with the basic grinding squat, the double-kettlebell front squat.

I am going to say 'simply' here, but the workload is incredible. Simply, the athletes do eight double-kettlebell front squats, then drop the weight to their sides and farmer walk for 20 meters, then do another eight squats and repeat until completing eight circuits.

That goal was often not met.

There are some hidden benefits to this combo. The athlete needs two kettlebells and never puts them down. The metabolic hit is accelerated by the grip work, the wrestling with the kettlebells and the sheer volume of carrying the load. It was this Eagle that made me think about the ideal combos.

There is nothing magical in the choice of exercises; it is the patterning movement of loaded carries mixed with the grinding movement of squats. For whatever reason, those two kettlebells are also a sign from heaven that this is going to be a hard workout.

Combo Two
The Pattern Movement of the Squat, Mixed with the Grind of the Hinge

Moving up the chart, note that the patterning movement for the squat—the goblet squat—works extraordinarily well with the grinding movement of the hinge—those Bulgarian goat-bag swings. This single-kettlebell workout can really stoke your fire. It doesn't have to be complex in numbers or structure, just try it.

And in fact, the goblet squat and the Bulgarian goat-bag swings lend themselves to the best workout I know, the ButtBurner 4000.

The ButtBurner 4000

Grab a kettlebell or dumbbell in the 25- to 60-pound range. Go lighter than you expect you might need. Now, give me a goblet squat. Then do a goat-bag swing. Now, do two of each, then three.

Here's the full workout—

> *One goblet squat and one Bulgarian goat-bag swing*
> *Two squats and two Bulgarian goat-bag swings*
> *Three and three*
> *Four and four...all the way up to 10 if you can.*

If you just go to fives, that's 15 reps of each exercise. Tens gets you 55 each and a lot of lost breath. It should go without saying, you need to build up on this one slowly. This combo will revitalize the entire lower body and teach you to really own both patterns, the hinge and squat.

The mistake most trainees make is to move too quickly to complex movements (the fun ones), but greatness resides in those who have the courage to master the patterns first, and then add complexity.

The simple patterns can also make for the most shockingly exhausting workouts. Try the ButtBurner 4000 sometime and see the value of simple, hard work.

Combo Three
The Pattern Movement of the Hinge, Mixed with the Grind of the Pull

The next movement has actually changed the way I teach both the hinge and the rowing motions for pulls. The wall-based Romanian deadlift (RDL) followed by a row seems to really protect the lower back—an issue for many lifters who row, including me—and lights up the whole back, from an inch below the knee up through the neck. That's a lot of muscles.

Be sure to feel the hamstrings stretching the entire time and focus on a quality pause (squeeze!) when the weight comes to the "top." That would mean this: With a barbell, pause when it touches your chest and with a kettlebell or dumbbell hold the position when the weight reaches your armpit.

Combo Four
The Pattern Movement of the Pull, Mixed with the Grind of the Push

The fourth and final combo as we walk the ladder up the lifts is to combine the patterning movement of the pull (batwings) with the grinding push (bench press or pushups). This is similar to the classic bodybuilding superset, but we're deeply protecting the shoulders. Many trainees tend to do far too many horizontal presses and totally neglect the opposite pull. That's also why many trainees have shoulder issues.

Thoughts on the Combos

The clever ones who look at these four combo packages have asked, "Why don't you mix planks with car pushing?" Now, that's funny, at least at one level, but, look, you'd better be fully planked when pushing a car or a prowler.

Recently, I gave the advice to someone at a workshop to mix car pushing with planks, but be sure to be going uphill. He didn't get the joke at first either, but the car will roll down over you while planking. And that's a bad thing.

These four combos—

> *Farmer Walks and Double-Kettlebell Front Squats*
> *Goblet Squats and Bulgarian Goat-Bag Swings*
> *RDL and Row*
> *Batwings and Pushup or Another Push*

—can be a training program in themselves.

The first two are clearly the best workout combinations I've ever used. The second two are more traditional bodybuilding movements, but work well with even the newest of trainees.

Now, the symmetry movements have an interesting metabolic hit in themselves. Maintaining symmetry, balance and structure seems to take the nervous system for a ride.

The following can be a taxing workout—

Suitcase Walk

Waiter Walk

Single-Side Squat

Suitcase Hinge (Suitcase Deadlift)

One-Arm-Row Plank using a TRX

One-Arm Bench Press

One-Arm Military Press

I strongly recommend *not* doing symmetry movements to exhaustion or in combination with other movements. There are some issues with safety, but, really, it's just counterproductive. Getting tired is not always the answer.

The Miracle of Pushups and Swings

Mixing ballistic movements with patterning, grinding and symmetry movements is advanced stuff, save for one combination: grinding pushes (pushups) with the ballistic movement of swings.

Josh Hillis has had marvelous success with mixing pushups and swings for his female clientele. An exhaustingly basic workout is the following—

Swings: 10 Reps

Pushups: 5 Reps

Swings: 10 Reps

Pushups: 4 Reps

Swings: 10 Reps

Pushups: 3 Reps

Swings: 10 Reps

Pushups: 2 Reps

Swings: 10 Reps

Pushup: 1 Rep

Two cycles of this can be an excellent tonic in the middle of training. Be sure to grab that free *Coyote Point Kettlebell Club* ebook from *danjohn.net* for plenty of other pushup and swing combinations.

Honestly, trying to mix ballistics with the other movements demands a high level of competence in patterning, grinding, symmetry and ballistic among *each* of the movements involved. You can get too far ahead of yourself and try to train ballistically without the proper foundation, especially in symmetry. When you drive a loaded bar over your head when you have a lot of symmetry issues, well, this is called a bad idea.

It's the same idea as dosage in medicine. Excessive amounts of Vitamin A can kill you, but you need Vitamin A. In the *Intervention* program, I ask how little can you do to achieve your goals, not how much.

Simple Strength:
A Few Months on the Park Bench

YEARS AGO, when I first met Pavel, he challenged me to do a 40-day workout. I followed his instructions to a T.

> *"For the next 40 workouts, pick five lifts. Do them every workout. Never miss a rep, in fact, never even get close to struggling. Go as light as you need to go and don't go over 10 reps in a workout for any of the movements. It's going to seem easy. When the weights feel light, add more weight."*

And I did exactly as he said. On the 22nd workout, alone in my garage gym, I broke my lifetime best incline bench press record, which was 300 for a single. Without a spotter, in a frozen garage, I incline-benched 315 for a double. All the other lifts went through the roof, and I'm as amazed now as I was then.

It's too easy. In fact, it's so easy, I have had to break it down into literally dozens of pages of articles to make it as simple as possible! And, the more I try to simplify the program, honestly, the more lost some people become.

I'm not entirely convinced I'm a genius, but somebody has to explain to me why I followed those instructions so easily and hoards of trainers can't seem to follow the concept without the obvious answer of me having an unrivaled intelligence.

Or, perhaps, I can just follow the rules.

So…I decided I had to create Simple Strength. I didn't want to, but I was exhausted explaining to people that 'three sets of three, adding weight each time' meant to do three sets of three, adding weight each time. My frustrations, I think, led to even more clarity.

Simple Strength for an Experienced Lifter

Let's start with an advanced experienced trainer who has never done any loaded carries. In three weeks I'll be proven correct, as the farmer walk alone will change everything.

There are a few rules before we begin.

Never miss a rep!

Follow the Rule of 10 (see pages 215-218) for the appropriate lifts for an advanced lifter. If patterning needs to be done, do it as often and as much as necessary, and use the rules of 15-25 for the appropriate half-body lifts (see pages 218-220).

Advanced warmups

5–25 Goblet Squats

75 Swings—sets of 10–25; really grease that hinge movement

1–5 Getups—half-getups are fine, or just some rolling around.

Week One

Day, workout number, sets and reps—workout details are explained below

Mon (1)	Tues (2)	Wed (3)	Fri (4)	Sat (5)
2x5	2x5	5-3-2	2x5	2x5

Week Two

Mon (6)	Tues (7)	Wed (8)	Fri (9)	Sat (10)
2x5	6 singles	1x10	2x5	5-3-2

Lifts for the workouts above—

Press Movement

Change the lifts every two weeks—make them the same, but different. Flat bench press, incline bench press and military press can be exchanged for each other after every two-week block.

Pull Movement

Either do batwings in combination with the press, two to three isometric holds for about 10 seconds every workout. Some people can skip this and get the work in from the other movements, like the swings or Olympic lift variations.

Hinge Movement

There are two options here, depending on need—either pick a deadlift variation and rotate it every two weeks—for example, thick-bar deadlifts, snatch-grip deadlifts, clean-grip deadlifts, orthodox deadlifts, Jefferson lifts or hack squats—or do kettlebell swings in the 75–100-rep range.

These options often cover the need for pulling, too.

Squat Movement

Again, ideally you'd alternate movements after every two weeks: Front squats, back squats, overhead squats, Zercher squats or safety squats are all fine.

Loaded Carry

Vary the distance *every* time, and probably the load, too, if you can.

Important Note

This might not necessarily be the order of the workout (from push to loaded carry). Some advanced trainers still need to do corrective work and still need to observe the issue that some movements are lagging behind and need more focus.

See Question Nine, Chapter 18, beginning on page 163: The issues—Are you willing to correct your problems?

The Workout Details
Two sets of five

It should be easy and be like your second or third warmup lift in a typical workout. The idea—the secret—is to get *this* workout to feel easier and easier.

Five-three-two

Do five reps with your 2x5 weight; add weight for three; then do a solid double. Make the double!

Six singles

I don't care how you do this, but add weight each set. No misses!

One set of 10

The day after six singles, do very light load for10 easy tonic reps.

Example workout for an experienced lifter

Week One

Monday, day one—

> *Incline Bench Press: 165 for five reps, 165 for 5 reps (300 max single)*
> *Thick-Bar Deadlifts: 185 for five reps, 185 for 5 reps (265 max single)*

These are the pull and hinge movements for an advanced lifter.

> *Front Squats: 185 for five reps, 185 for 5 reps (405 max single)*
> *Farmer Walks: 105 with each hand, 100 meters out and back (three stops)*

Day two can be heavier or lighter depending on mood and feel. The important thing is to show up and get the movements in. If one day is too hard and compromises the next day, that's fine as long as you lighten the load and continue getting the reps without compromising speed.

Day three should begin with the rep five number from the usual 2 x 5 workout, then add some weight for three, and finally add some weight for two. Be sure to get the double.

Most people on the simple strength program find this workout is the test for how things are progressing. The weights begin to fly up on the double, and that's good, but stop there. Remember, this is a long-term approach to getting strong—don't keep testing yourself. Save the big effort for, well…never.

Day four and day five are the most confusing days. Again the load on the bar depends on how you feel. If the efforts feel easy and light, nudge the load up.

Here's the secret (again): The goal of this program is to gently raise your efforts—the load—on the easy days, so the bar feels light. If you start out lifting a weight, say 205, at one effort level and in a few weeks you're lifting 245 at the same perceived effort and speed, *you're stronger.*

After a day of rest, day six is going to feel easy, and it should. Get the reps in.

Week Two

Day seven has a simple rule: Do six singles adding weight *each* rep. It can be five pounds or 50, depending on how each single feels. It's *not* a max effort on the last set, it's the sixth single. If the loads feel heavy, just add five pounds. If the bar is flying, add more.

If you come from a background that insists every workout be Armageddon, day seven will be confusing. The goal is to determine the load based on how the weight feels. If it pops right up and feels light, toss on the plates. If it doesn't, respect today and realize you're going to have plenty of opportunities to get stronger in the future.

Day eight is a 'tonic' day, the way we used to use the term. Go really light and just enjoy 10 repetitions. It can be as light as 40% of max, or lighter if you want, and use the movement to unwind after yesterday's heavy attempts.

Day nine is often the day when people see the reasoning behind the program. This is the day when the weights often seem far too easy. That's the sign of progress in this program. I remember actually thinking I misloaded the bar and had to double-check my math as the bar seemed far too light to be right.

Day ten is sometimes the day when people test themselves a little, and this can be fine as long as you feel like going after it. Again, don't miss.

Here's the confusing part—

**You don't need to go up
every two weeks, every workout, or, really...ever.**

Just keep coming in and trust in the process.

Week Three
Option One

The original program Pavel designed demanded a repeat of weeks one and two, three additional times. Oh, and it works well. By week five, I was a machine on the lifts and broke lifetime personal records, smashing my incline bench press record by 15 pounds for two reps, not just a single, and crushing my old thick-bar deadlift record, going from 265 to 315. This is staggering improvement.

Option one is to merely follow Pavel's plan and keep on keeping on.

Option Two

I like this one more for most athletes. You make small changes to the movements, from bench press to incline bench press, thick-bar deadlift to snatch-grip deadlift and front squat to back squat. This is Pavel's 'same, but different' approach. Those small changes seem to keep enthusiasm high for the entire eight weeks.

Option Three

I have a few athletes doing this and I believe (well, maybe 'hope' is a better word) this is the better option for speed and power athletes. It's both a deload week and week filled with more metabolic challenges.

Day One
Push Press or Push Jerk

Rule of 10—five sets of two, adding weight each set, is a great workout.

Litvinovs

After doing a hinge or a squat movement, either sprint, sled or work the prowler immediately after finishing. In a gym setting, this can be difficult, but I've done this outside with great success with just a kettlebell and a hill.

Day Two

Left arm only!
Waiter Walk
Suitcase Walk
Single-Side Squats—kettlebells are best
Suitcase Hinge—deadlift

One-Arm Row using a TRX or similar device
One-Arm Bench Press
One-Arm Military Press
Reps, sets, load, time and every other factor… it depends!

The idea is to push the stability and symmetry muscles and movements. There's an odd metabolic hit to these moves as you'll sweat a lot more than expected.

For example, this can be done with a single kettlebell in a park—which is wonderful by the way—and you can challenge various aspects of training and get a good workout while also practicing mastery of body position and dynamics.

Doing just one side also frees up your mind a little. It's pretty obvious what you'll be doing in a few days, so you can experiment a bit and play at the edges of tension and relaxation as you train.

Day Three
Push Press or Push Jerk
Rule of 10—five sets of two, adding weight each set, is a great workout.

Litvinovs
As on day one, after doing a hinge or a squat movement, either sprint, sled or work the prowler immediately after finishing the first movement. In a gym setting or outside, and, of course, outside is best.

Day Four

Right arm only!
Waiter Walk
Suitcase Walk
Single-Side Squats—kettlebells are best
Suitcase Hinge—deadlift
One-Arm Row using a TRX or similar device
One-Arm Bench Press
One-Arm Military Press

Week Four

At the beginning of week four, you'll mix up the variations in the basic movements—push, pull, hinge, squat, loaded carry—and progress along using the same rep and set template as weeks one and two.

Weeks one and two are repeated four times total. Option three would be a 12-week program.

After finishing the program, fully assess your mobility, basic strength levels and the program vis-à-vis your goals. I'd suggest maybe an FMS screen and blood tests, too, if costs and availability aren't an issue.

Going All Out: A Few Weeks on the Bus Bench

Now, let's deal with the other great confusion in this plan: Yes, you can train much of the year with just five movements repeated over and over with the subtle variations of three options. I suggest doing this up to as many as 10 months a year!

Let me stick to this one example first: *10 months a year of simple strength and two months a year of bus-bench training.*

This is actually what I think just about anybody in Quadrant Three should do, from Grandma trying to lose fat to an elite thrower. Yes, that means you, Mr. Highland Games thrower who emails me for secret training information, but if you're still not sure, see Chapter 8, beginning on page 63, for a refresher on the quadrants.

Those other two months are when you should light it up. These are the times for the bikini beach workouts, the intense, full programs and the hard lifting. Skinny throwers, do *Mass Made Simple* (also see the book if you're a skinny football player). The other throwers might do two life-altering three-week rounds of the Big 21—see *Never Let Go* or my articles at *danjohn.net* for details.

The problem with most of us is we have this idea that we have to train always and everywhere with our foot pushing hard on the gas pedal. I've trained many athletes, literally in the thousands, in a camp experience where we train four times a day. We also have our meals prepared—all we can eat—and most of us stock our fridges with extra food and drink. Nearly every time I do this, someone asks—*Wouldn't it be great to train like this year-round?*

No.

Sadly, I used to think so!

These intense camp experiences have a great value in raising intensity, polishing technique and expanding us. But, then we need to go home and train as we normally do using these new insights. I used to tell the campers, and I regret this, to make a camp experience at home. Now, I tell them to take a little time off and use their journals as a tool to mine the camp experience.

Then, adapt and grow.

Take a calendar, ideally a 12-month view-at-a-glance variety, and honestly cross out those months where life is not going to allow you to train at the highest human levels. For accountants, look at March and April as crossed-out months. For parents, all the boxes from about Thanksgiving to New Year's are full. For athletes, the height of your season is *not* the time to ratchet things up—the hay is in the barn, or whatever cliché you like to use is appropriate here.

We have this work ethic that somehow we feel we're sinning unless we train at maximal effort each and every workout. That's simply not how the body works. We need to ramp it up at times, yes, no question about that! However, keeping the gas pedal down at all times leads directly to burnout. Find appropriate weeks and months to really attack what you need to do, but don't be afraid to ease off when you need to.

Or, better I think, why not just plan this? Successful programs build in a deload week. The simple strength program accommodates deloading either by having those fun 'option three' workouts or just going in to the weightroom and taking it easy.

Some people, like me, struggle with easy days in the weightroom. I really need to be away from the fun and camaraderie of the gym and its strange ability to make me train hard and stupid no matter how smart my programmed workout was supposed to be. Plan those months, weeks and days far ahead. Use your brain to find those times when it's obvious you either can't or shouldn't train to the edge. You still need to train and watch your food and drink intake, but use these training windows as time to maintain most of your qualities.

Others have told me they can actually do four months a year of bus bench, goal-focused intense training. I applaud that, but try this approach—

- ✦ Two months of simple strength or variations of it
- ✦ One month of a 'Do This!' bus bench program

This actually works well for many people. Remember, as you come to the end of an easy training cycle, you will be looking ahead to some hard work, or what you perceive as hard work. When you come to the last week of a program that has you squatting heavy for a hundred-plus reps a week, you will be brightly looking forward to the end of it.

Chapter 26

The Intervention Approach to Diet and Nutrition

For much of this work, I have ignored diet and nutrition, a real pillar of the *Intervention* approach to working with people. Yes, I know that you, gentle reader, know exactly what to do in this area, but let's talk about the great chasm between what we know we should eat and how we actually do eat.

I took up the study of heroes in college. Part of my work in my first masters degree was studying *Beowulf.* Now I know many readers consider this punishment, but to this day, the work gave me an insight that still propels me.

In the speeches in the story of *Beowulf,* warriors speak in the pure present. They mention the past...in passing, and rarely look beyond the next fight. If a buxom woman offers her charms before the Battle of the Seven Mountains, our hero doesn't stop her to comment that he needs to finish his creatine and five ounces of chicken and those three almonds.

Kings, however, speak in a way we would hope visionaries would consider. Yes, these are the dull speeches that make up much of the book with a short review of the history that brought us here, a quick summary of the present situation and a hopeful look ahead. To see it perfectly, whip out a copy of the *Gettysburg Address* and note that Abe Lincoln followed the model perfectly.

"Four score and seven years ago," "Now we're engaged in a great civil war," and "The world will little note, nor long remember what we say here," are not only some of the finest poetry in English, but provide a model for great toasting on any occasion.

Warriors live in the pure present. Kings live in a situation where they need to look backward, as well as forward to assess what to do next.

And, this is the issue for me: I'm a coach.

I dig deeply from those rich veins of gold I've mined for over four decades to give you a few gems when you're ready. I know, too, sooner than later you'll be glad I hand them out sparingly. Like the clichéd quote goes, "When the student is ready, the master appears."

I'm certainly not saying I am a master at many things, but there's a touch of wisdom one gathers from all this time under a bar.

In my travels, I notice many strength and fitness athletes tend to look at food as a warrior would: Here it is, I eat it. I'd like to challenge you into a new relationship with food—look upon it as would a king in *Beowulf.*

Let's start by reexamining our relationship with food. You have to understand I'm not judging one approach as good or bad, but it helps to know your focus and your goals.

First, consider the warrior's approach to food.

The Velocity Diet is Warrior 101. Fourteen bottles of protein, a shaker and some supplements is pretty much all you need for the next few weeks. When someone asks, "Is it good for you?" you'll reply, "Have you seen my abs?!"

In other words, for fat loss—what I consider only the second hardest thing to do with the body—gain lean body mass is the winner here—the winning approach is living in the pure present: *Be a warrior.*

Today, as intermittent fasting, also known as IF, and other methods of long fasts followed by intense eating have become so popular, it might not shock you to read about eating one meal a day.

About five years ago, I had the opportunity to work with some people at a military workshop, and almost all of them were doing intermittent fasting. Due to the remote location, we could only find one place open when we broke for dinner, a popular fast food place with a red and gold clown as its salesperson. To listen to five guys who had not eaten all day but had worked hard for over 12 hours order at the eatery was worth a video. I'm sure every mother and father in the place shielded their children's eyes. It was a sight to behold, as burger after burger was flushed down.

As one guy explained it to me, "I only eat once; I have to eat a lot."

For the record, these guys were all ripped and in great physical condition. It may have been frightening, but it worked.

That's the warrior mentality.

Look at what you see here—

There is not a lot of cooking in eating at fast food places or drinking six protein shakes a day. Now, truly, if you wish to follow a plan like this kind of fasting, learn how to use a crock pot or BBQ grill. One thing you will notice is that quick fat-loss plans often leave little for the taste buds to enjoy.

This isn't the way your mom taught you to eat.

That's true. It isn't. The Warrior Way probably has a number of things Mom doesn't want you to do. But, let's make this clear: For fat loss and short-term goals, I'm not convinced anything works better than to deal with it with the vision of a warrior. Getting ripped, truly lean, is not about taste buds, satiety or gourmet cooking. It's about food as a tool...and a lot of hunger.

And you can do it for short periods throughout your life. This, my friends is a bus-bench approach to eating. And, like bus-bench workouts, they had better work!

For all other goals and any kind of lifetime approach, I recommend following the King's approach.

I have some advice for you. Recently, a quote from my book *Mass Made Simple* became a *Facebook* status line several times, and in the world of blogging was the finisher for quite a few rants about diets. I sum my insight about all things diet, nutrition and supplements with the simple phrase—

Eat like an adult.

Honestly, seriously, you don't know what to do about food? Here's an idea: Eat like an adult. Stop eating fast food, stop eating kid's cereal, knock it off with all the sweets and comfort foods whenever your favorite show is not on when you want it on, ease up on the snacking and—don't act like you don't know this—eat more vegetables and fruits.

Really, how difficult is this? Stop with the whining. Stop with the excuses. Act like an adult and stop eating like a television commercial. Grow up.

I know as well as anyone the emotional connection we have with food. At a wedding, don't ask me to count drinks because I am trying to remember the last part of the Chicken Dance. At a funeral, especially of someone close to me, I might indulge in a few pastries and I am not going to feel awful about my lousy carb choices.

In fact, I started crying at the end of my first meal during the Velocity Diet. For those of you who forgot already: the V Diet is six protein shakes a day. That's it! No food., save one meal a week!

On my beloved meal that Saturday, I pushed down a t-bone, some eggs, some toast and a sweet-tasting Scotch. My wife asked what was wrong and I responded, "What the hell?" Realizing I wasn't going to eat again for seven days brought out a trickle of tears.

I get it.

I get why no matter what you did in elementary school, you deserved and got a piece of candy because you're so special. It reminds me of what they tell students at top universities, "Look to your right. Now, look to your left. Every kid around you was a straight-A student in high school, was the class president and probably Valedictorian. Get over it."

Every time you succeed in life does not call for several extra rounds of beer, a salutary doughnut and high-fives for everyone. I've always admired great athletes—Barry Sanders comes to mind—who score a touchdown, goal or point, and just keep moving along. It's your job, so get over it.

If trying to make a lifetime impact on lean body mass as a goal for you, you need to stop the cycle of emotional eating. If you have issues with emotional eating or binging or purging, you need far more help than I can offer, but this is also a glorious insight into the King attitude—

> *The demons you have in your past*
> *are changing the way you look today.*

I've always equated bigger with better. More load, more volume, more food.

And, my friends, that catches up to you. I literally have to unpack that skinny kid out of my brain and redirect my diet and training to something a late-middle-aged man can do.

So, how can I help?

First, what is your philosophy of food? I'm serious here, what is your basic approach to shopping, cooking and packaging food?

Elaine St. James has made an industry out of living simply. My favorite of her books is *Simplify Your Life.* Her first point on health is to simplify your eating habits. She and her husband decided to simplify life and discovered making an honest effort in simplifying meals also led to a healthier diet.

She settled on two principles. One, no surprise here: Eliminate the junk food. She goes on to discuss other options, like to always split a restaurant meal when you go out.

Second, they also wanted fewer calories, and less fat and cholesterol. One thing she chose was to drink water rather than all the rest of the options laden with cheap calories.

On the path to simplicity and cutting back the time devoted to making meals, St. James discovered that she and her husband simply looked better.

Now, if everything I've just written is appalling to you, the antithesis of everything you believe and think about, well, you might just be a warrior. Sooner or later, though, you have to shift gears and gather a long-term focus.

Most people tend to know what to eat. St. Jean's ideas are all well within the range of normal. There's no mention of HCG, exotic herbs or excessive measurements of anything.

Step one to the kingly approach to eating is to have a long-term focus. We all know vegetables, lean protein and fresh water are probably the best choices, meal in and meal out, for the rest of your life. If you hover around those choices for the bulk of your meals, you'll be fine.

You know this.

The second step is to work with your personal and perhaps odd relationship with food.

We have a barbell issue with most people when it comes to food. The barbell is an excellent way of imagining a graph with highs on both ends and lows in the middle. If I tell you to eat all the vegetable soup and salad you want for the rest of your life, you'll find a dozen excuses not to eat that much.

On the other hand, if I tell you to give up a single item, perhaps carrots, well then, we will have a major fight on our hands as you try to convince me you can't live without carrots. Even if you haven't had a carrot in the past 20 years, you will still crave carrots. From this, we will drift back into that middle area of foods like chips and sodas and breads and cereals, and graze ourselves up to a nice level of obesity.

Step one is to begin to have a long-term view of how you approach food. Step two is to understand that for most of us, being omnivores, we're going to struggle somehow with food restrictions.

The third issue with the Kingly approach is cooking. What's funny is that I've met a lot, and I do mean a lot, of people who have read my work. Many of them have never cooked a meal because, and there's nothing wrong with this, their moms do all the cooking.

Then they tell me they embrace the Warrior Spirit. And, while that might be true, but as often as you yell, "Ma, where's the meat loaf?" you need to start looking at a different relationship with food.

In the strength world, there are many extraordinary strongmen who are also brilliant cooks. Marty Gallagher, who trained Captain Kirk Karwoski and Ed Coan, two great names in powerlifting, is a famed name in cooking. I'm no expert on BBQ, but the point is important: A lot of ribs, chicken, beef and pork prepared well and eaten seems to make you big and strong.

To eat like a king, you need to shop like a king, too. Many fat loss experts recommend that we take two days a week, say Sunday and Wednesday, to skip the workouts and use the time to do nothing but shop and prepare meals.

That's a kingly approach to food. And it seems to give the best results for fat loss that stays off.

So, yes, the warrior approach to food is absolutely correct. Sometimes. Like its good friend the bus-bench workout, you need to balance this into your year, decades or life.

For the bulk of our lives, however, I suggest learning a relationship with food in which you plan, prepare and consume with vision of satiety, leanness, fullness and long-term success. You probably already know the answer.

Yes, you know: *Eat like an adult.*

The Quadrants of Diet and Exercise

I AM CONSTANTLY AMAZED at the great amount of discipline and free will people have just before they start a life-changing program. Of course, this lasts, usually, about a day. Years ago, I published an article about a diet I was doing for a short time and a guy challenged every reader on his blog to follow me—and him—into this great journey.

He quit after one day. That's about right for most people. Part of the problem is that all too often, people will decide to do a Warrior Diet (like a Two-Week Cayenne Pepper Liver Cleanse) mixed with a bus-bench workout program. By now, you might be glad you read the earlier chapters to understand that sentence!

Let's look at our four options in my second favorite way of seeing choices—after continuums, of course—the quadrants of diet and exercise.

	Park Bench Workout	Bus Bench Workout
WARRIOR STYLE DIET	Tough Diet Reasonable Workouts	Tough Diet Tough Workouts
KING STYLE DIET	Reasonable Diet Reasonable Workouts	Reasonable Diet Tough Workouts

I think by using the words reasonable and tough, I show my hand a little bit about this point, but I have yet to come up with better. I feel like I need to wave my hands around and say 'you know' a lot when I explain it. But, you know, reasonable is repeatable, doable, and believable.

Tough is going to make you wake up at night worrying about the workout or diet.

It shouldn't be a shock that I suggest reasonable diets and reasonable workouts for most of your year and life. This would work really well if we were all automatons.

You know…like I'm always trying to remind you that what you ate is much more an issue than this marvelous imaginary world of 'what you are going to eat.' The Red Queen of *Alice in Wonderland* would disagree with this, of course. I think most people fall in love with her great insight that's far from my view of things—

"Well, in our country," said Alice, still panting a little, "you'd generally get to somewhere else—if you run very fast for a long time, as we've been doing."

"A slow sort of country!" said the Queen. "Now, here, you see, it takes all the running you can do to keep in the same place. If you want to get somewhere else, you must run at least twice as fast as that!"

Most people in the fitness industry slide over to the Warrior Style diets and bus-bench workouts. Honestly, few of us have the internal motivation to take on burning both ends of the candle. The Red Queen would love to see you run faster and faster to go, usually, nowhere and, come to think of it, this is exactly what treadmills and exercycles do. I wrote extensively about this in *Never Let Go*—few of us have the free will, time and opportunity to be so disciplined to do both tough diets and tough workout programs at the same time.

Now, of course, *you* are the exception, as I am usually told. A very drunk person once said to me, "I'm all about discipline," both hands filled with food and drink. And, no, I was not talking to a mirror. That time.

I can certainly see periods of tough diets and reasonable workouts for many people. I've done this with various diets from Atkins Induction to the F-Plan Diet. This approach works well for tightening up after a holiday or a vacation. There are a myriad of three-day, twelve-day and two-week blitz diets on the internet, and new ones appear daily. It might sound counter to what you've been reading, but when someone says, "I'm doing the Three-Day Blitz Diet," I support it as best I can.

Sometimes these little experiments can get a person back on the path. Losing five to seven pounds in a few days is certainly enough reward for the sacrifice of eating much less for a bit. This is not a lifestyle, but you will find that many religious traditions have this kind of communal fast built into the yearly cycle, too. It works, for a little while.

Reasonable diets and tough workouts are the basic template for athletes. There comes a time of year when we need to do The Big Push. It's 'all hands on deck' time and we need to bring up the qualities necessary to succeed. It's nice to be in reasonable shape going into this ramping process, and this is a fact missed by many. Being in pretty good shape most of the time trumps being on the razor's edge of perfection.

As Mark Reifkind reminds us, "The first step down after a peak is a cliff." These are strong words and well worth thinking about when you decide to go on some epic training program while eating only 500 calories a day. Oh, you can do it, but should you? For more on this, read *Jurassic Park*. Just because you could do something, doesn't mean you should.

Every question in the *Intervention* toolkit is designed to get you to think about training—and later, diet—in a reasonable, appropriate way. Literally, the 10 questions are set up to cover the basic point: *This is you.*

I want you to think about and address relationships, community involvement and living your life well beyond the next few decades.

Not long ago, I was in my living room defending the idea of the spiraling of goals, question number three from the toolbox.

"It won't work; you're telling me I need to make more time!"

The ensuing discussion highlighted the problem with most diet and exercise regimes—the person was in the gym up to three hours a day! The problem was this: Of those three hours, most of it was spent foam rolling, doing dozens of correctives, dynamic mobility moves and assorted stuff before getting on the treadmill for his cardio. In other words, he was in the gym a long time doing everything, but, in so many ways...nothing.

I took him to Dave Turner's Hercules Barbell Club. Precisely at 10:00 o'clock, we started jumping jacks and Dave's long but fast warmup circuit. We then grabbed sticks and went through the basics movements of lifting. Next, we went to the barbells and did 26 sets of exercise under Dave's eagle eye. We put the equipment away, gathered together to chant the mottos of the Club and walked out the door.

It lasted one hour. My friend, who could barely walk the next day, told me he understood where all those hours of spending time with family and community were going to come from in his new schedule. Reasonable doesn't mean easy.

As John Powell always says, "I said it was simple, not easy."

Reasonable looks so, well, *reasonable* on paper. In practice, it is often the hardest thing we can do.

If I've convinced you that reasonable diets and exercise programs trump a few days or weeks of insanity, you'll be far further ahead. I've done my best to show what a prudent approach to health, fitness and longevity can provide, but the rest is up to you.

Jerry Seinfeld said it best—

> *"But the pressure is on you now. This book is filled with funny ideas, but you have to provide the delivery. So when you read it, remember: timing, inflection, attitude. That's comedy. I've done my part. The performance is up to you."* ~Jerry Seinfeld, *SeinLanguage*

The pressure is on you now. The performance is up to you.

Coach Stevo Case Four

I hope you stay with *Intervention* long enough to see this for yourself: *Intervention* is so simple, it feels like cheating, and clients might even feel like it is. Your clients will doubt the system will work because it's rarely hard. But if as a coach you can find the patience to help your clients find the path and have the courage to keep on it with kindness and grace, you will have given them all the tools of the *Intervention* toolkit and they will look back and wonder how they ever got lost in the first place.

She makes it look too easy. Maybe she's on steroids or something. But she isn't huge or anything. She's just, I don't know, toned or whatever. But I've never seen her in the gym for more than, like, 15 minutes. She just picks up those kettleball things, swings them between her legs, squats them a couple times, then pushes them over her head like some powerlifter. I don't get it; she's doing it all wrong. I'm on this damn elliptical for like, ever, and she barely breaks a sweat! I bet it's genes. I bet she was never fat.

"Actually, I was fat."

"What's your secret then? I've been trying to lose weight forever."

"There's no secret. I just do what I can; try to keep moving and get a little stronger."

"Is it those kettleball things? Are they better than the elliptical? I'm doing boot camp, too."

"Well, I mean , I guess it depends on what you're looking to do."

"I'm trying to lose weight. Should I try those kettleballs?"

"If you think you'd like to. But really I just picked something and stuck to it. You know, I keep trying to better at it, but I don't let it rule my life."

"That sounds too easy."

"It's not easy. It's really hard to stick to something."

"Will it work faster than the elliptical?"

"I don't know; I know getting stronger worked better for me."

"I lost a bunch of weight when I started, but now I don't think I've lost more than a pound."

"Yeah, that's kind of how it worked for me. It happened slowly. Not at first, of course. But as I got better at moving and kept things reasonable, I found it a lot easier to keep going. Then slow wasn't so bad. I just had to keep moving forward and let it happen."

"How long did it take?"

"You know, I don't even remember. One day I just said, 'Oh, I guess I'm here now.'

"Where?"

"You know. Here. Where I want to be. Happy with myself, I guess."

"Do you know a coach who could help me with that?"

Chapter 28

Concluding Thoughts

I DON'T KNOW WHY people have come to think they need insanity to progress, but I feel like I break hearts when people realize that reasonable trumps insanity every time. To keep the surprises to a minimum, I start my *Intervention* workshop with the following spoilers.

Rosebud is his sled.

Luke is Darth Vader's Son.

Harry kills Voldemort.

Frodo lives.

Reasonable trumps insanity.

If any of these are spoilers for you, I apologize. But reasonable workouts done for a lifetime, peppered with some intensity and mastery, are always going to trump insanity done briefly.

The Five Principles seem so simple when I first lay them out. They're so simple; I sometimes feel the need to go into long, rambling explanations with charts, graphs and stats to explain these truths.

Now, I just stick to the plan—

- Ask the 10 questions
- Listen to the answers
- Apply the principles

The results speak for themselves.

Know your goal. Understand the path. Stick with the basic principles. Let success happen.

Index

About the Author

DAN JOHN has spent his life with one foot in the world of lifting and throwing, and the other foot in academia. An All-American discus thrower, Dan has also competed at the highest levels of Olympic lifting, Highland Games and the Weight Pentathlon, an event in which he holds the American record.

Dan spends his work life blending weekly workshops and lectures with full-time writing, and is also an online religious studies instructor for Columbia College of Missouri. His previous books include *Never Let Go, Mass Made Simple* and *Easy Strength,* written with Pavel Tsatsouline.

The companion DVD for this book, *Intervention,* was filmed in 2011 and is available through *optbooks.com.*

You can keep up with Dan via his website at *danjohn.net.*